The Ultimate Supply Teacher's Handbook

Also available from Continuum:

100 Ideas for Supply Teachers, Julia Murphy
100 Ideas for Primary Supply Teachers, Michael Parry

The Ultimate Supply Teacher's Handbook

DEBORAH HUGHES

continuum

Continuum International Publishing Group

The Tower Building   80 Maiden Lane
11 York Road   Suite 704
London SE1 7NX   New York
                            NY 10038

www.continuumbooks.com

British Library Cataloguing-in-Publication Data
A catalogue record for this book is available from the British Library.

ISBN: 9–7808–2649–6263 (paperback)

Library of Congress Cataloging-in-Publication Data
A catalog record for this book is available from the Library of Congress.

Typeset by B[...] [...]
Printed and b[...]   nin, Cornwall

Contents

INTRODUCTION

Supply teaching is something I always vowed never to get into. Having witnessed some unpleasant encounters between classes and supply teachers, as a student and as a student teacher, my mind was very firmly made up to only ever take permanent teaching positions. More recently however, with a number of years' teaching experience under my belt, I turned to supply teaching as a lifestyle choice and found the diversity of experiences on offer both stimulating and liberating. For me, the return to pure teaching – without the meetings, report-writing, administrative chores and general long-term responsibility – unexpectedly suited my lifestyle. Choosing when and where to work, the shorter working hours and travelling between different schools, meeting a range of colleagues, appeals to my way of working. I teach in both primary and secondary schools; teaching subjects across the curriculum to a variety of classes is very interesting.

Professionally I have been able to widen my knowledge of schools, a perspective that is very tricky to gain by being exclusively at one school. As a supply teacher you are in the unique position of being able to compare systems and procedures and learn from 'best practice'; as such even a short spell doing supply should enhance your professional development and is an ideal opportunity to seek out and market yourself to a school you wish to work in on a permanent basis.

There are of course the downsides. Even the best behaved of classes can pull out all the stops in order to liven things up when they realize they have a supply teacher, and the reality can be that just containing a class and ensuring no one gets hurt is in itself a success.

There is no doubt about it, teaching supply can be a sink or swim affair (you only have to take a glance at the supply message boards on the internet to see how disheartened teachers get); the luxury of bedding in a class is just not an option – you have to be prepared, and be prepared to think fast and act fast and have a whole catalogue of tricks and strategies at your disposal!

I'm still not sure that I would have had the nerve to have cut my teeth doing supply as a newly qualified teacher (NQT) but those that do so successfully – either because they have chosen to do so to suit their life or due to the lack of teaching jobs in some areas – learn quickly how to keep a class on task and will gain invaluable experience that will stand them in good stead should they choose to pursue a permanent post in the future.

This book is aimed at anyone interested, or in fact already involved in supply teaching and may be useful also to cover supervisors, a role becoming more popular now in schools. It deals with ways of getting into supply teaching, a typical day and tricks and tips for dealing with the dilemmas and situations thrown up from day to day. Every school is different with differing intakes, a diverse chemistry of staff, varying forms of leadership, expectations and ethos; therefore it is impossible to aim this book neatly to match the experiences of any given supply teacher. I have instead tried to work using a continuous spectrum often using the worst-case scenario as a point of reference. This means that it can sometimes appear that I have only captured the very negative elements of supply teaching and the worst aspects of student behaviour. In fact, I have had very many positive and rewarding experiences as a supply teacher, but my philosophy is that it is better to be prepared for the worst that can happen – anything else then is a bonus! I have heard teachers in charge of cover euphemistically describe to supply teachers new to a school that classes are 'fine', just a 'little lively' or contain a 'couple of colourful characters', which, it turns out, is teacher-talk for 'it's complete chaos in there!' I think it's better to be realistic than to suddenly find yourself in the eye of the storm.

I have included the tips and tricks that I have learned over the years as a teacher, a head of department, an advanced skills teacher (AST) and a supply teacher. I have always been open to ideas from all ages and experiences and hope that the sometimes very detailed strategies will be seen as practical and insightful – some I found indispensable as an NQT; others I have picked up since starting supply. They all seem obvious once you've learned them!

The Ultimate Supply Teacher's Handbook aims to help you to prepare for all eventualities, so that at the end of the day you can leave school feeling happy in the knowledge that you have managed the situation as positively as possible and that you can look forward to the new challenges ahead.

1

WHY SUPPLY?

There are many different reasons for opting to teach supply: lack of suitable jobs; a way of finding the school to suit you or for a school to discover your talents; a flexible way of fitting around a family, partner or other interest; a career break or even preparation for management. More and more supply teaching is being considered not as a period of unemployment but as a broadening of experience.

Finding a school to teach in permanently

With a shortage of jobs in some areas, some teachers and NQTs find themselves taking on supply teaching jobs as a necessary means of providing an income. If you are new to the profession or perhaps new to an area and looking for a full-time job, supply is a great way to see a number of schools from the inside. Anyone who has ever on interview been shepherded rather rapidly round a school, pausing at only the classroom where students are behaving well, will understand the importance of seeing the real picture. Equally, proving yourself on supply is an excellent way for schools to pick up candidates who perform well in the thick of it – not just in the artificial conditions of an interview, teaching your model lesson to a class of hand-picked, docile and amenable pupils or, conversely, attempting in vain to tame an awkward set in the space of 20 minutes. Through supply you can get to know a wide range of schools or, if you're aiming to be on the books for a small number of local schools, you can offer your service directly to get a proverbial 'foot in the door'.

Part-time teaching to suit your lifestyle

Supply presents infinite opportunities for flexibility. Tired of seemingly endless meetings, report-writing and the increasing burden of paperwork or even just staffroom politics, supply teaching is a convenient means of enjoying teaching without the extras. More and more teachers are opting to work two to three days a week, either as a gentle way of easing into retirement or to allow space in their life for other things. Parents wishing to fit around a family or those wishing to develop another business or hobby also opt for supply as a more manageable way to keep life balanced. The hours are shorter; preparation (unless taking on a short-term contract) is minimal; staff meetings, parents' evenings, and irksome paperwork are no longer necessary. Add up the hours spent doing all those things other than actually teaching in the classroom – and it could well be more cost-effective to be a supply teacher!

Professional development opportunities

How many schools do we get to see in a career? As a supply teacher you get to see a whole variety of schools in context. There are no airs and graces put on for supply staff – you see the place, warts and all. This is a priceless opportunity for professional development. Student teachers learn a great deal about teaching by simply observing various teaching styles, picking up excellent tips and also learning from any 'mistakes'. The position of supply teaching is very similar; the focus is more on the school and its procedures rather than on individual teaching styles.

Some teachers feel anxious that on their CV a break from a permanent job might reflect poorly, but in fact it is surprising just how much can be learned in a relatively short amount of time. I once met a headteacher who concurred that her spell of supply teaching had been one of the best preparations she could have undertaken before taking on her headship. Simply visiting schools to introduce yourself will provide a very broad insight into how a school presents itself to outsiders; working in them, meeting a range of practitioners and practices is an almost unbeatable form of in-service training.

There are various ways of becoming a supply teacher: you can apply to be listed as a supply teacher of a local authority (LA) and approach schools in person; you can join a local authority pool; or you can use the services of an agency. Your choice depends very much on your background in teaching and why you have chosen to take on supply work.

Agency or personal approach?

Deciding on whether or not to go with a teaching agency is very much down to your personal circumstances. If you have been teaching for a while and are known in the area you wish to teach, you may have enough contacts, or a good enough reputation, to go it alone and approach schools in person to get onto their supply list. Some schools actively seek to staff their own supply lists, preferring not to use agencies, while others will deal only with agencies. Some counties operate a sort of pool system and others run their own 'in-house' version of an agency, providing a better deal financially for schools and supply staff. There are so many different systems in operation that you will need to research what avenues your particular area has to offer. If there is a particular school in which you would like to work, it's worth checking their policy for taking on supply teachers.

The advantage of being a free agent is that you get paid without a cut being taken by the 'middle-man'. It also means that you can choose in which schools you would like to work. Granted, agencies will send you back to schools where you get on well, but if they are sourcing teachers to a large number of schools, the personal touch is not always possible.

The downside of being an independent freelancer is that you will have to do the initial groundwork, marketing yourself to various schools. If you are dependent on regular work, an agency might be the more secure option – with so many schools on their books they should be able to provide opportunities to work on a daily basis. If you choose to go it alone, on the other hand, it may take a while to build up a portfolio of schools that are willing to offer you work on a regular basis.

Think about how many days a month you are hoping to work and why you have chosen to do supply. If you are looking for a couple of days a week, at a local school where you can build a relationship with staff and pupils, or you have a good track record in your area, you will be better off approaching schools directly. If you need a steady income, want to find a school where you'd like to work full time, or you wish to work intensively for chunks of time interspersed with bouts of travelling or resting, then an agency is a more practical option. However, remember that if you are ultimately looking for a permanent position at a school, contracts can hamper this transition. Before signing up with an agency, make sure you establish exactly what your agreement with them entitles you and your school to do. Schools often have to agree not to 'poach' agency staff without paying quite a large financial penalty. There may also be clauses in your contract that prevent you from taking work from a school that the agency introduced you to without a significant time lapse – in which case working independently might be your best option in the long term.

Agencies

Supply teaching is unrecognizable from what it used to be, even within the last few years. As any agency official will tell you, things have changed rapidly.

Supply teachers used to be sourced chiefly through local authorities (LAs). Today, with the demand for teachers so great, recruitment agencies, endowed with a wealth of experience of providing temporary workers to business, have stepped into the educational arena to work either alongside local authorities or instead of them. Some agencies such as Eteach.com are specifically aimed at the supply market; others are recognizable high-street names such as Reed, Select, Capita and Hays who recruit teaching staff for both day-to-day and longer-term assignments. Some agencies are set up by local authorities with the intention of placing temporary staff accurately within the authority and offering better financial terms for both teachers and schools.

Frequency of assignments

There are of course advantages and disadvantages of going down the agency route – you really need to be clear about why you would like to do supply before deciding. The obvious benefit is that agencies are in the best position to offer you regular work, especially once you have established a good relationship with your local office and they know what kind of assignments best suit you.

With hundreds of schools on their books, agencies can cover a much wider field than you could manage on your own, so in theory you ought to be able to pick up work regularly pretty much straight away, provided you are available at the drop of a hat. Once you have proved yourself to be a reliable and valuable member of the team, you will be more able to pick and choose when and where you would like to work. To begin with you will need to be regularly available – you are less likely to get called if you often turn down assignments. You can belong to as many agencies as you wish (as long as you are motivated to fill out forms for each and to be interviewed for each); in theory this gives you an even wider field, though again agencies are only likely to call you if there's a good chance of you being willing and able to work.

Getting you started quickly

Agencies have the advantage of removing the bother of marketing yourself by taking care of all of the paperwork centrally. This means that you can get onto the books and into the classroom fairly quickly, as opposed to having to present yourself at various different schools or spend hours mailing your CV to staff in charge of cover. In some cases, agencies promise to get you into schools while your Criminal Record Bureau (CRB) check is being processed – the agency carries out a number of other background checks – useful if the alternative is waiting 4 to 8 weeks without work.

Some schools and authorities will *only* use agency staff these days. This might cost the school more on the face of it (schools pay over the odds for agency teachers), but it can be cost-effective if it saves a member of staff time finding and vetting suitable candidates, a thankless and sometimes impossible task. If this applies to many of the schools in the area where you wish to work, your only option may be to sign on with an agency.

Pay

One of the most obvious disadvantages of agencies is that the rates of pay (which generally work out to be much lower than nationally agreed teaching salaries) vary between agencies. It can be quite difficult to ascertain how much you will be paid until you have been interviewed.

Most agencies pay a daily rate on a weekly basis, though this may alter if you choose to take on a longer-term assignment. Some agencies pay a flat fee per hour (this can vary, depending on the area). This may suit candidates with little or no teaching experience, struggling to get placed in schools, but it may not be so desirable for experienced teachers, higher up on the point scale. Other agencies will recognize and honour scale points but many determine their own rates; they take into consideration factors such as your scale point, the strength of your references and your career history. If you develop a good relationship with an agency and they ask you to take on an assignment at a school far away from you, you may be able to negotiate travelling expenses, particularly if the school is keen for you to work for them.

Before committing to any contracts, establish, in writing if possible, the hourly rate. If you are opting for an agency (as a way of banking on regular work), if they are paying a significantly lower daily rate than a school would if you were supplying for them directly, then it might be prudent to work fewer days initially until you have built up your reputation and are able to bring in work more frequently on your own. For example, with some agencies paying only £80 per day rather than say a possible £140 at LA rates, then it's preferable to work independently for two days and devote the third to promoting yourself elsewhere.

Remember that once an agency has introduced you to a school, any work you undertake for that school – even if they approach you personally – will have to be agreed by the agency and the agency will continue to take a cut of the fees unless the school buys out the contract.

Another downside of agencies is that although in many ways they make life simpler – like switching your gas and electricity bills to one supplier – in other ways they make life much more complicated. Choosing an agency can be like trying to select the best mobile phone deal with a range of confusing and difficult-to-compare tariffs.

In my experience, some agency staff demonstrate excellent interpersonal skills; others become very irritable when asked 'awkward' questions concerning pensions, sick pay, legal representation and contractual restrictions regarding future employment directly with schools. I suspect that offices with staff who take the time and effort to answer questions end up signing teachers because of the honesty and respect shown. It is undoubtedly a difficult job trying to please both client (the school) and contractor (you), but you should feel confident that any agency you are going to sign up with has your interests at heart too. Of the various agencies I made enquiries with some were very happy to answer my queries and others were decidedly cagey. You can interpret that as you wish: perhaps the staff simply weren't well-informed with reference to their company policy or perhaps the terms don't appear attractive, but unless you are in a position of absolute desperation, such concerns should be seriously weighed up.

On the whole, LAs allow you to continue making contributions to your teaching pension and offer legal representation. One agency I spoke to told me that there was an allegation against me, I would immediately be suspended and would need to seek the advice of my union. Another explained that the agency would cover the costs of court proceedings but that it would advisable for me to be in a union, which would fight the case for pay should my contract be suspended.

Sick pay and holiday pay is also a variable. Most agencies include holiday pay within their daily rate: if you are being paid £90 a day, roughly £12 of that will be holiday pay – this puts your daily rate in a different light. Sick pay is paid by some agencies but not by others. Some will pay it if you have worked a specified number of consecutive days for that agency (and perhaps even the same school, as it is the school that will ultimately foot the bill); others offer only statutory sick pay after a three-month period of illness. All employers should honour paternity and maternity leave – these are government payments to which every employed person is entitled.

Professional development opportunities can be helpful in keeping your CV fresh and up to speed. Some agencies offer in-service opportunities either in the form of materials to read or by running courses after school or during holidays free to agency employees. These are usually set up to meet the demands of schools and in keeping temporary employees up-to-date with the latest initiatives; they are worth attending if you are looking for full-time work and wish to keep your CV current. When deciding on an agency, ask what in-service provision they offer and what courses have recently run. Incidentally, schools will also often allow supply staff to attend in-service sessions, so keep an eye out for anything that might be relevant and ask if you can join in.

Contractual obligations

Many supply teachers don't fully comprehend the consequences of signing up with an agency until it is too late. If one of your reasons for turning to supply is to open up your opportunities to find permanent work, make sure you read the small print in your contract before you commit. Unsurprisingly, having invested time into attracting and then vetting you on behalf of schools, agencies are reluctant to let your services go without fiscal reward. This usually works by the agency creaming off a chunk of what the school pays them for your services. If however a school decides they would like to offer you a long-term position, you are contractually obliged to let the agency know. The agency will either allow the school to employ you via the agency, in which case you are still technically working for them and are therefore fixed into their rates (not the professional scale that regular teachers are being paid and you've been dreaming of); or the school will be required to pay the agency a sort of fixed penalty notice to buy you off the agency's books. Although a school may well be prepared to do this (it will have saved money on advertising, filtering candidates and interviewing), it may make you a rather less desirable option. If you have only visited the school once and happened to spot, or have your attention drawn to an advert for a position there, then this is unlikely to present a problem – but it is always worth clarifying this point before you start.

Signing up

Call around a few agencies and ask questions before deciding which agency to go with. Details of agencies are available in the *Times Educational Supplement* (TES), on the internet or in the telephone book, or a colleague may recommend an agency. Talk to other supply teachers – word of mouth is a valuable form of feedback.

When you call the agency, it is usual to give a brief history of your career and answer a few questions concerning the kind of work you are looking for – day-to-day assignments, long-term cover (or even, in the long run, a permanent position); which sector (this can range between nursery to further education (FE)); and which subjects. If the agency is able to accommodate your wishes and you seem to be a suitable contender, you will then be asked to attend an interview. Either beforehand or actually at the interview you will be asked to provide any or all of the following:

- your CV
- qualification certificates
- proof of GTC/DFES number
- current CRB certificate or a cheque (£36)
- 2 forms of ID: passport, birth certificate or driving licence
- National Insurance number

- proof of address (usually a bank statement, utility bill or credit card statement)
- P45 (or you will be asked to fill in a P46)
- your bank details
- name and contact address of 2 referees (usually your previous head and another; for NQTs a tutor and perhaps teaching practice school)
- 2 passport photos.

Going it alone

Agencies are the easy option if you would prefer someone else to do the legwork or if you are getting very little return applying to schools personally. Agencies do offer a service but it is one you are paying for in terms of lower pay and fewer rights, as you hand over control to them. If you are in a position to, it may be more rewarding both financially and in terms of personal choice to go it alone.

Doing your research

One of the benefits of becoming an independent freelance supply teacher is that you have the privilege of deciding where you would (and definitely wouldn't!) like to work.

Your first task is to make up your mind where you wish to teach. This might revolve around schools where you have previously worked, schools where you have contacts or schools that fall into a specific geographical area – for instance a 10-mile drive or easily accessible bus routes. Buy a map of the local area and take the time to mark on possible schools so that you can easily calculate estimated journey times and see which are the easiest to reach.

It's worth drawing up a schools database, including the name of the school and headteacher, telephone number and address, perhaps even information such as number on roll. Start by plundering your local directory such as Yellow Pages, and supplement any extra information from the internet or by phoning the school. Some counties issue lists of schools and their details to registered supply teachers. To make sure your approach is more than just a circular, you will need to know who to address in the first instance. For primary schools, your initial contact should be addressed through the headteacher; for secondary you will need to find out the name of the person in charge of organizing cover.

Registering as a supply teacher

This is a relatively straightforward procedure though by no means a uniform one. Having decided where you would like to work you will need to register with the LA as supply staff. On the whole it is better to do this before approaching a school – the school will not be able to offer you work until you have been cleared by the county, accepted on the county payroll and have obtained CRB clearance. Some counties have a specific section to deal with supply staff; others are incredibly difficult to get hold of and can involve relays of voicemail tennis; some offload their supply contracts to an agency in which case you might find yourself being transferred directly to an agency operator. Generally, you will be asked to fill out forms detailing your experience, listing referees and outlining what kind of supply jobs you would prefer to undertake. For all but one of the schools I work for regularly I have registered with the county. For the other school, which draws from its own list of supply staff instead of the agency staff provided by the county, I filled in an application for the school directly, and provided my own CRB disclosure certificate (see page 19).

Marketing yourself

Schools are busy places, with little time to devote to poring over lengthy letters and CVs, so your introduction has to be snappy. Before you print off and send the last, updated version of your CV, consider revising the format to a hybrid of CV and promotional leaflet: quick and easy to digest. A business card with your photo and contact details is also a useful device – it is a handy size to display on the office noticeboard (often placed next to the telephone) and a cover organizer is more likely to phone a teacher to whom they can put a face, rather than to a random name; these are easily and cheaply available on the internet.

Remember to include easily accessible contact information on your CV as well as your qualifications and employment history. Think about what skills and qualities the school will require of a supply teacher and incorporate a short section describing how you can fit that bill. Where possible, use an open reference, pithy quotes from referees and a photograph – but avoid making your 'brochure' too cramped; it needs to be easy to read to survive the filtering process. Less is more: select the pertinent experiences of your working career rather than an exhaustive portfolio of everything you've ever achieved; consider what skills a school will be looking for and include those of yours which are relevant in a snapshot. Once you have the interest of a school, you can then expand on any aspect they want to know more about. Do include all employment history – gaps only spark suspicion.

Make a personal appearance

Ensure your information gets to the right person and is not fast-forwarded into the wastepaper basket with all the other bumf which regularly clogs staffroom pigeon holes – go in person to the school. Primary schools are often particularly appreciative of this gesture. It shows you are willing to put yourself out and the school can put a face to the name. You may also have an opportunity to look around.

If possible, avoid showing up unannounced; it is far better to phone ahead and arrange a time to drop off your 'application'. That way the headteacher has the option to meet you. Don't be disheartened if the headteacher does not feel the need to meet you – organizing supply is a job often undertaken by office staff.

Having met you, and possibly informally assessed your suitability at that meeting, the person in charge of cover will be more willing to call on your services, rather than that of a faceless name on a letter.

Keep your visits short, unless invited for an informal chat or a guided tour, and keep questions to a polite minimum. You need to create a favourable impression; it is best to gently reinforce any of your selling points (for instance a track record of working with difficult pupils, a speciality in PE, SATs experience) and let the school representative ask the questions. When they show an interest in inviting you to work there, you can clarify further details.

With larger primaries and secondary schools you will need to make a more specific appointment to catch the person in charge of cover. First call ahead and find out the name of the relevant person. A chat on the telephone, followed by personally delivering or sending your details will be enough, but if you can get a tour of the school, then so much the better.

Organizing visits

Now you are a freelancer, every day not working is a day unpaid so if possible arrange a number of visits to schools on the same day. This enables you to travel around the area using up one day rather than several. Use your local map to mark the location of the schools and plan a route. That way you won't spend the day doubling back on yourself and you can indicate to a school roughly when you will be popping in. You might also find yourself passing schools that somehow escaped your original information-gathering session – it is always worth popping in on the off chance. Take spare copies of your CV/brochure/business cards in case such an opportunity arises.

Dress professionally. Although you are technically only on an informal visit, first impressions last. Consider any chats an unofficial interview.

Have your covering letters and CVs ready in envelopes addressed to the appropriate person. This makes it easy to leave information in case the person you wish to see is not available. It is also worth having a few spare copies to hand, should office staff request a copy for their files. Responses can vary: at some schools, particularly primary, headteachers are keen to vet applicants; at others administrative staff are charged with the duty. At secondary, deputy heads and senior staff are more likely be responsible for cover. The rule of thumb is to be polite, respectful and professional at all times, to all staff – you never know who is evaluating your suitability. Don't be surprised if, following a conversation about who you are and what you've done previously, the person on the front desk asks whether you are available a week on Thursday.

Take a copy of your school database with you; mark off when you have delivered your letter. It's a good idea to make a few brief notes about the school as soon as you come out; if you are visiting a number of schools previously unknown to you, it is surprisingly easy for names and places to get mixed up in your mind as the day goes on. Jot down who you spoke to, how you felt and any extra information you gained which might help you to smarten your profile appropriately – for instance, the school may be looking for someone who can play the piano, has experience working with autistic pupils, can teach resistant materials or will be available for a maternity or paternity cover in a specific year group or department later in the year. Have your diary with you: it is amazing how many times you can find yourself in the right place, at the right time and be offered some days there and then.

CRB check

To work in any school you will need to provide proof of a recent Criminal Records Bureau (CRB) enhanced disclosure certificate. This is a background check carried out by the local police authority on behalf of a school, local authority or agency. You have to fill out a form that is then processed – this can take between 4 to 8 weeks to complete. Agencies generally look after the paperwork for you as part of their application process. If you are going to work as a freelance supply teacher, go into one of the schools in the county where you are planning to work, taking with you various forms of identity; get validation of your identity from the head or senior teacher. The local authority will provide you with the appropriate form when you call them.

Once you have been cleared, your CRB certificate entitles you to work for up to three years before needing renewal. However, some authorities or agencies will only accept a CRB disclosure certificate that is less than 12 months old when you approach them. If you have a break from teaching of three months or more you will be required to apply for a new certificate. If you live on the county border and are planning on working in more than one county you may need to complete a CRB disclosure form for each one; some local authorities will accept a current certificate procured for a neighbouring county but others won't. Some authorities do not keep records of CRBs, which means that any change in your status (supply to permanent or long-term cover) may require yet another disclosure procedure. I worked for an authority for 13 years on the strength of my initial disclosure certificate; then I went through about four in six months when I first started supply because I was working in three different counties and then took on a long-term maternity cover! Some counties will pay for the disclosure and others require supply teachers to pay for themselves; most agencies will look after the paperwork but do require candidates to pay for the check. The certificate is valid for three months; it may become void if your employment lapses within the county or agency over a three-month period. Then you may be required to re-apply for a CRB certificate – though if you are registered with a county and working regularly with them its validity should remain intact for the three years.

Claiming pay

If you are used to a regular salary rolling straight into your bank account, working as a supply teacher can come as a bit of a shock. Filling out claim forms, either directly to the school or with the agency is a must if you want to be paid on time. As agencies have all your details on record, the system is slightly easier in that you will be required to fill out a time sheet. Working independently means that you may have to negotiate a variety of systems.

My favoured system is where the school fill out all the forms and you just have to check and sign – usually the office staff are so efficient it is impossible to leave the school without being reminded that you need to claim and as a result you always get paid on time! At others you may be given the forms to fill out – have information such as your National Insurance number and DFEE number to hand. In some cases you will need to actively seek out the cover office and ask for the forms and then be responsible for remembering to hand them back in. Orders for payments from schools have to be submitted by a certain date in the month and if you miss it, you may end up waiting for another month before being paid. Schools or agencies will need to take bank account details at some point – generally this information is then held by either the agency or the county.

If you are working for more than one county, you will be required to declare one as your main employer for tax purposes. It may be worth seeking the advice of an accountant or the Inland Revenue – who are incredibly helpful in such cases – to ensure that you have been allocated the correct tax code.

Employment status

As a supply teacher you may find yourself self-employed or setting up a company, even if you're the only member of staff! Consult an accountant and business adviser on the best solution for you – it depends on your individual circumstances and the work you wish to pursue. Most supply teachers don't do this, but there may be financial benefits that make it worthwhile.

Insurance

Depending on the route you choose to take and your personal circumstances, it may be worth seeking advice from a trusted financial adviser regarding income protection insurance. As a full-time, permanent member of staff you will be covered for illness and accidents, but contracted employees have much less protection. There is also the possible issue of damage to your property, accidental or otherwise. Find out from your agency, union and school or LA what insurance cover you are entitled to and who provides it.

Pensions

The provision to make superannuation contributions is not usually available through an agency. If you are registered with the LA you will need to let the finance office know that you would like contributions to be deducted at source. Again, it is worth discussing pension options with a teaching union and/or an independent adviser.

September

Bear in mind that, if you are only planning to supply to a small number of personally selected schools – as opposed to the whole raft of establishments offered by an agency – September might not be the most fruitful month. Training courses tend to run later in the year (particularly in the summer term), in order to allow staff to settle their new classes in the autumn, and perhaps take advantage of exam leave at secondary. Coughs, colds and various bugs have a propensity to strike after autumn half-term when the weather has taken a turn for the worse and staff are more tired and run down, and prone to catching anything going – September is likely to be a quiet month. There may of course be maternity and paternity leaves or posts that couldn't be filled on offer, but if you are banking on a wage it might be better to take the agency route or extend a summer job for another month. Alternatively you could enjoy the beautiful weather that always follows the long summer break and enjoy a fabulously priced holiday while the 'kids are back at school' – a luxury generally denied to teachers!

Protecting ourselves

As supply teachers, working in a diversity of environments, constantly negotiating varying expectations and a range of levels of support, we are probably the most vulnerable professionals in schools today. Yet surprisingly few supply teachers choose to join a union.

On a practical level, we are most likely to be interested in the day-to-day issues we that might affect us such as health and safety affairs or allegations made by students, rather than the long-term arbitration between the profession and the government. However, it is essential that we do not neglect to consider what we would do should some kind of dispute arise.

As with all staff we need to be conscious of the situations in which we might find ourselves and do our best to avoid potentially difficult situations. Most staff these days are mindful of ever being alone with a student and are all too aware of the impending hazards that say practical subjects might present. While it is possible to be cautious – and vigilance grows with experience – we are never able to guarantee that we can guard against all eventualities. I taught PE for 10 years without a major injury. However, in one school, in a matter of weeks, I had four girls (between Year 7 and Year 11) who managed to bat the ball into their own face during games I was umpiring. They were simple accidents that could have happened to anyone, anywhere, and fortunately were seen as such, but as a supply teacher I felt extremely exposed in spite of being in a school where I was well known and respected for my experience and professionalism. As a full-time member of staff we develop a reputation and a familiarity with a school and parents, but as a visiting supply teacher it is very easy to feel like an 'outsider', and very open to criticism.

In terms of protection, there are four options: join a union; seek written assurance from your teaching agency that when you sign a contract with them they will protect your legal rights; start your own savings fund to finance a solicitor or lawyer should you ever need one; or close your eyes and cross your fingers.

Joining a union

As teachers we rely on unions to protect our rights, defend sensible working practices and represent us should we find ourselves in legal difficulties. Unions are very experienced in these matters and work exclusively on behalf of their members. Your agency may well advise you to join a union on top of any legal protection they may offer.

None of the major teaching unions have a package specific for supply teachers – you will be classed as a teacher. As such all of the usual cover will apply to you with the exception of the ability of the union to negotiate your salary. All of the unions offer a reduced rate for supply teachers working part time, though what is defined as part time varies from union to union.

What support does your teaching agency offer?

When signing up with a teaching agency, always check what legal support is offered; don't be swayed by claims that there have never been any problems or believe that your rights will be protected without seeing that it is written into your contract somewhere. Protection varies, so find out exactly what provision is made

- If you end up having to go to court following an incident in school, will the agency cover court costs and if so for how long?
- Will you be covered should you be suspended from a post while a case is pending? For the majority of teachers this is an unlikely scenario, but it is better to be informed than to find out should problems arise.

Remember that agencies reap huge rewards for hiring you out to schools and ought to be looking after your interests; but remember also that they have split loyalties and will want to remain on good terms with the schools.

Legal fund

It may sound flippant, but some people actually do set up their own form of insurance. I once met a husband and wife who were both teachers and had decided to bank the money they would have paid a union with the intention of using it to pay a solicitor should they ever need one. This meant that they forfeited all the other perks and specific expertise offered by unions but they had decided that their own solicitor might more personally represent them. This is a bit of a Russian roulette approach – for the majority of staff school life ticks along with no real problem, but if circumstances dictate that you need legal representation you need to weigh up whether you will have the access to the educational expertise and unlimited funding that a union will be able to offer? Possibly not.

Eyes closed, fingers crossed

Many people neglect to join a union on the premise that they can't afford the extra cash; others decide that the school they work in seems a decent enough place without much trouble and the chances of winding up in some legal wrangle are negligible. This is one way of looking at things albeit a slightly ostrich-head-in-the-sand-approach, not to be recommended. It's a bit like crossing a road without looking – if you can't see the cars they're not there! Schools are brimming with accidents waiting to happen and it is as well to err on the side of caution, keep your eyes open and look both ways!

Checklist

- If you opt to work via an agency do your research. Find out about:
    - pensions
    - holiday pay
    - sick pay
    - legal representation
    - pay and conditions
- If you are going it alone, decide where you wish to be based and register with the county or the school directly:
    - make sure you apply for a CRB check in plenty of time – some can take months to come through – your agency or LA will provide you with the paperwork.
    - draw up a database of potential schools then make contact initially by telephone and – if possible – in person.
    - market yourself effectively with an appropriately tar-geted CV or brochure.
    - visit schools to introduce yourself.
    - remember that September may be a frugal month if you freelance independently.
    - consider consulting an accountant or business adviser about the best business status to suit your conditions, particularly if you intend to take on other types of work.
    - consider taking out income protection insurance.
    - find out what legal protection your agency provides.
    - join a union.

Try to be aware of the students' perspective when they first meet you. Younger pupils may be quite daunted by the fact that their own teacher is away; for older students you may be the third or even fourth cover teacher they have seen that day, or even the latest in a stream of different teachers they have been 'palmed off with' for that particular subject. Try to sympathize with their situation – they don't know yet how great you are going to be! Conduct yourself in a firm but friendly manner

Your name

Remember to introduce yourself. At primary level it's difficult not to, but at secondary it's amazingly easy to let it slip in the initial flurry of trying to get the class under control. If in doubt, write your name on the board.

Opening activity

Depending on the situation, choose the right opening. With some classes, (usually primary) settle the class with a chat about who you are; perhaps tell a short story about your day so far: spend a little time to get to know your charges.

A colleague of mine always starts with 'Bin and Bring', where he talks about the things that have happened to him today that he needs to bin, because those things won't help him learn (being worried about his cat or excited about the weekend); and which things he is bringing with him to help him to learn (a smile, a positive attitude or a good pair of ears); he then asks each of the class to do the same. He also explains that he will forget their names and the class come up with ideas as to how they can help in the smooth running of the classroom. Any variation of 'show and tell' is also a nice way to bond with the class.

Time doesn't often allow such an approach at secondary and it may be better to adopt a business-as-usual approach; the less deviation from the norm the better!

Be honest

Be honest about your situation. You are there for a short spell and will need cooperation. The students' way of testing is to make the same demands as those of the regular teacher and expecting you to meet them. Rather than trying to fix everything, you sometimes just have to explain that you are not able to solve a problem and suggest that the students offer a reasonable solution.

Building a reputation and being professional

In order to be invited back, you need to make an impact and be noticed above other supply staff. That means going above and beyond, and maintaining a strong sense of professionalism.

Although more and more teachers are turning to supply teaching out of choice, there is still a stigma attached to the job. Many take the attitude that supply teachers do not have the commitment to the profession. To that end, supply teachers and cover supervisors can be rather marginalized. That said, good supply staff are highly valued and schools will go out of their way to retain them – it is well worth building your reputation for being professional.

Dress appropriately

At secondary smart/professional will be expected; at primary smart/casual is more accepted. For both, you need to wear comfortable clothes and footwear. Be geared up to step in and teach PE or drama at primary, and at secondary be prepared for long walks across the campus. Be prepared for rain too; you don't want to appear like a drowned rat thanks to a sudden, unexpected shower and a long hike from the art block to your science lesson.

Arriving early

Make sure that you arrive at in plenty of time – 30–45 minutes early depending on how well you know the school and how much supply teaching you have done. There is quite a lot to do before you even appear in front of a class. See the extra time to prepare as time that will make your day run more smoothly rather than viewing it as unpaid time.

Set off with plenty of time to spare, particularly if you are unfamiliar with the school and the area. If you are driving, check the route on the internet and take account of rush hour traffic, one-way systems or roadworks. Remember that finding the school is one thing but locating the correct car park and actually finding a space is another. Incidentally, if there appears to be the perfect parking spot completely free right at the front of the school – beware before you slot yourself in and skip into school – it is probably reserved for the head! For public transport commuters it's worth trying to make the earlier train or bus, at least on your first visit; arriving late on your first assignment there will not create a good impression.

Once you are at the school, you will be required to sign in and collect any ID, keys and passwords needed for the day. You will also meet briefly with the cover organizer to run through your day and, ideally, introduce you to key staff. If it is possible, attend any morning briefings that might be relevant.

Arriving early also allows you to have a quick walk around the school and become familiar with the site and the whereabouts of any classrooms you where you will be teaching.

Gossip

It is sometimes difficult to suss out the lay of the land when it comes to staffroom politics. As a supply teacher, you may be left well alone in the staffroom or you may find yourself welcomed into a group of staff or faculty group over break and lunchtimes. Join in and enjoy the company but avoid getting involved in staff politics. Be diplomatic with your opinion, whatever you think about other staff or the way the school is run. Refrain also from bad-mouthing pupils, even if you have had a difficult day – some of their parents may well be in the room!

Never pass judgment on other staff even if you feel that their lesson planning has left you in the lurch or their support has been less than helpful. If it has become a serious issue, there are proper channels to follow; moaning about them in the staffroom, even if other staff are doing so is not appropriate. Find an understanding senior member of staff and put forward your case diplomatically by explaining your position rather than fingering someone to blame.

It should go without saying that it is not professional to make derogatory comments regarding other teachers in front of pupils either. Students may laugh and even appear to accept you more to begin with, but they won't respect you for it. Respect for you will come because you are a good teacher, certainly not by putting someone else down to make yourself look better – even students know that is a cheap shot.

Similarly, refrain from sharing personal information with students. Tell amusing anecdotes but sharing tales of nights out and low-level swearing are not appropriate even if you are closer in age to the students than many members of staff. Your students will recognize this as a weak ploy to curry favour even if they encourage it.

Finding the cover!

Many schools have introduced universal cover sheets to be used by all members of staff to provide a sense of uniformity across the school. This is a whole school format that outlines details such as class and size, subject, year group, starter, main activity, plenary, resources, etc. There is often a section for the supply teacher to feedback. When they are used they are usually very helpful. Unfortunately, hastily scribbled notes on scraps of paper can be all too common! This is especially inconvenient for cover supervisors, who are paid to deliver activities set by teachers rather than concoct a 'one-off', and for teachers covering beyond their specialism.

Finding plans can also be a bit of a game. Some teachers leave them firmly taped to the desk with multiple copies of the original safely disseminated to colleagues and office staff. Others leave neatly labelled pocket wallets on desks with clearly organized instructions and pockets allocated to store collected work. Sometimes plans are left with the head of a department in the department office, or can be found in the teacher's pigeon hole (away from mischievous pupils or the chaos of the office) or with the cover office. The key is to find out! Chances are there will be a school procedure explaining where plans should be left, but don't be surprised if the interpretation of it varies! If the school doesn't appear ruthlessly efficient, keep an eye out everywhere: check pigeon holes in the morning if you have been told that they might be there (though rifling through people's personal space might not go down well!); look out for heads of department; check the rooms that you are due to be teaching in later. The earlier you can get to see the plans the better.

Teach!

Your job is to teach and even if the class are getting on well, it doesn't look good for you to be indulging in a little 'me time'. Reading the paper, texting, knitting or finishing a chapter of your book during a lesson is not what you've been paid to do, even if you don't think much of your rate of pay!

Leave classrooms spotless

Leaving the classroom spotless (even if it wasn't before) leaves an impressive 'calling card'. Try to get your classes to pick up and tidy as a matter of course. If you forget to pack up early enough to get the room back as it was, it really is your responsibility to pop around and pick anything up. Leave books stacked neatly (open to the page where possible), equipment returned tidily, the floor and tables clear, and chairs up if you have overseen the last lesson of the day. Students can sometimes be reluctant to tidy up but are always more willing to help if they see you chipping in. Let them know that the class will leave *when* certain criteria have been met; if they have any complaints about not being the person that dropped whatever needs picking up, acknowledge that you know that they aren't personally responsible but that you would like them to help tidy up. Please, thank you and a smile go a long way here.

Reinforcement

Respond according to the behaviour you want to see, and to the behaviour you don't want. Expect that students will test you more than once to make sure your boundaries are clear. Having somebody out early on for swearing or calling across the class often sends a shot across the bow and proves that you have the confidence to follow up on poor behaviour. Be consistent with your responses and the class will soon learn your way of operating. Similarly, using rewards for correct behaviour, from a thank you or quiet well done to a team point, merit or 10 minutes playing a game, will help to develop the kind of behaviour you want to see. As teachers this is the bit we often forget, or believe that we shouldn't have to thank or con-gratulate behaviour that ought to see 'as standard'; but it is these boundaries that pupils feel assured by and ultimately respect.

Offering a reward

Offering a reward can be a useful lever in getting work done, but is best used when you know a class. If you start off by bargaining with the class for work that even they regard as work that should be done, you may come across as malleable and open for negotiation. Before you know it, you will be under pressure to offer rewards for the completion of a short section of work or for 'being good' (a thinly disguised threat that the group might be bad if they so chose!). I have seen teachers haggling with classes who have announced that they will do some work if they can watch a video. When introducing a reward, start by saying that you're thinking of offering one but only if things seem to be going well; make sure it's known that the prerogative for a reward is yours, and that if you feel you are being hassled it won't be an option.

Being yourself

'Never smile until Christmas'

I'm not sure I agree entirely with the sentiment of this old teaching adage. Although there is undoubtedly a kernel of wisdom there, it is easier to ease up than regain control. I think students really do respond to strong personalities and do like to see a person who is happy in themselves as well as strong in their own convictions. I have seen teachers have nervous breakdowns because they are trying to be strong, harsh, ruthless leaders, shouting because they have been advised that they need to in order not to appear weak. In reality, they are kind and caring but playing the role has never allowed them to expose this and they have spent their days of teaching in a constant pitched battle with students – miserable and stressed.

There is no doubt that as teachers, particularly as supply staff, we need to be strong but that doesn't mean we need to lose sight of who we are. Be yourself, smile, tell jokes and funny stories (yes, before Christmas!), but be fair and consistent and always follow through. I think that a much wiser maxim to live by in education is

> *'Do as you would be done by, speak as you'd wish to be spoken to, treat as you'd wish to be treated, respect as you'd wish to be respected.'*

What I love about students is that they are a pretty fair-minded bunch on the whole. They may whinge and whine but they will take a sanction if they know they've been in the wrong and that you have administered it fairly. They are quick to forgive if they believe that ultimately you have some respect for them. What they don't like is sudden surprises, changes in expectation, a feeling that they are being personally persecuted rather than justly punished. What they also want to know is that you are in this for them and that you have their interests at heart. Sometimes this does take time to get through, but I have never met a student who wasn't willing to change their mind, unlike many adults.

So be yourself, make a bond with a class, with the individuals who make it up; accept them as developing beings, not quite perfect but willing, with the right guidance, to improve. Learn their names, laugh at their jokes, show an interest in their interests, in their opinions, in who they are. If you are good at telling stories spend 5 minutes entertaining them. If you play guitar, take it to school and play a quick taster at the beginning; promise more at the end if they've done what you ask. Have high expectations of their behaviour and of their work, even though you are only with them briefly – this shows you respect and care about them. And don't be offended by their mistakes.

View your progress relatively. The best piece of advice I think I have been given was that as long as you can see progress, no matter how minor and how gradual, you are winning. It's tough as a supply teacher but over time, you will see changes in attitude and behaviour; students will come to accept you, to greet you, to trust you. It does take time.

Taking the right approach

Teaching, like all jobs, is about using the right strategy at the right time. Although there are tried and tested ways, it's best to remain flexible and have a mix-and-match set of approaches to suit the situation and the school. It is easy to miss the mark by trying to be 'pally' with a group who are looking for you to show them strength and end up with the class running all over you, or to alienate a relatively pliable class in the first few moments by barking out orders when they are used to being spoken to in a mature and considered manner. Look at how other classes behave and ask teachers to share effective strategies if they have time. Never be fooled by a teacher who makes the job look easy – a lot of hard work will have gone into priming that relationship.

If there are problems, stand back and assess them. Survey what appears to be a noisy class before wading in to complain that they are making too much noise. Very often it will be just one or two pupils causing most of the havoc. If it is just one or two characters catch their eye and tactfully redirect them to work. This will save you having to deal with an audience and the confrontation it brings. Sometimes a loud and aggressive intervention from the teacher just helps to spread disruption amongst previously on-task students. If the noise is just generally loud, listen in to conversations; you may actually find that they are discussing work rather than gossiping; although the noise level is high, you may realize that pupils are taking down chairs, getting out equipment, handing out books and that the class will naturally settle, without your involvement in a minute or so. If activity is more geared towards pushing, shoving, yelling taunts or making social arrangements across the room, then intervene by stopping the whole group and explaining what you want to see done in the next minute. If you have the presence and volume, stop the group straight away. I usually wait for a slight lull and signal that I am unimpressed and waiting by raising my eyebrows or looking at my watch. With rowdy classes I have used the whiteboard to communicate, explaining that the lesson will start when the class are quiet; it will run its duration from that point and I chalk up minutes owed to me. With groups who are still motivated by incentives, I award credits to those sitting ready to start.

At secondary, being stern and brusque tends to work better in more disciplined schools where back-up will be swift and evident, and with younger year groups who are slightly less savvy. In some cases the no-nonsense, take-no-prisoners method can sometimes transport you straight through the 'testing zone'.

At schools where you can see that discipline has been much more difficult to manage, a strict approach might simply court confrontation. In these situations, humour and tolerance is probably more likely to win the day, if not the hour. Obviously still aim to create the best learning environment possible and not accept very poor behaviour, but bear in mind that you are not going to achieve fast results. Students may be distrustful; accepting you won't be easy. Ultimately, the best way to find out what your group will respond to, is to try different tactics and learn from their responses.

Bad days

There will be good days and there will be awful days, just like any job. When you've enjoyed a day of sunshine and games, or a series of cooperative and good-humoured classes and you get to skip out of the gates without the addition of marking, planning or staying back for parents' evenings, it's easy to see why supply teaching can offer the best aspects of teaching. On bad days, without regular colleagues to share your woes, it can feel like a very lonely job. It's easy to forget that establishing yourself as a permanent teacher can be equally harrowing, and that students are seldom perfect.

The more you visit a school and your face becomes familiar, the more you will become accepted by both staff and students at a school; and as you become *au fait* with procedures and routines and learn from your experiences, the more perspective you will gain on the job. Situations and circumstances sometimes conspire – try not to take things personally and if you can muster it, smile in the face of adversity.

Checklist

- Try to consider the students' perspective: at primary they may be upset that their regular teacher is away and at secondary you may be in a long line of supply teachers they've had today.
- Remember to introduce yourself, and at the very least write your name on the board.

- If it helps to settle the class, spend some time telling them about yourself and finding out about them.
- Acknowledge your limitations.
- Build a quality reputation and make a concerted effort to do the job as well as you possibly can.
- Dress professionally.
- Arrive in plenty of time.
- Be diplomatic at all times.
- Always try to follow the instructions left even if they are patchy; use your back-up plan if all else fails.
- Actively teach.
- Leave the classroom as tidy (if not tidier than) you found it.
- Be fair and consistent.
- Offer incentives.
- Be yourself.
- Be prepared to try a number of approaches.
- Accept that there will be bad days.

4

LOOKING AFTER
YOURSELF

Schools can be incredibly energy-sapping places and it is easy, within a short amount of time, to feel completely drained. Be aware of this and limit your output; we all want to do an excellent job, but performing at 100 per cent all of the time is just not possible.

Choose your battles

While it is good to show yourself to be part of the team, it is not necessary to get involved in every dispute. By all means intervene in the corridor if an event requires, but don't feel the need to pick up on everything. Ties being straightened or shirts tucked in are fine to make a point of in the classroom, but out of class you could undermine your own authority by insisting on something which consequently gets ignored, or even worse brings on a confrontation. Obviously if something dangerous is happening, then it is your responsibility to step in, but for minor rule infringements it is much better to leave it to a permanent member of staff unless you are so well known at the school that you will be able resolve the issue with little bother. It is when we get sucked into situations beyond our control that valuable energy, better spent elsewhere, is depleted.

Similarly, in the classroom pick your battles. If it is difficult getting a class in, seated and listening, then gum, trainers and uniform issues can be dealt with later. There is no point in spending the afternoon in a pitched battle with a group of Year 10s over uniform; much better to focus them into actually completing some work. However if the school is on top of such issues and classes are generally well behaved, then being pedantic will signal to students that your standards are the same as anyone else's. Teachers who are positive but insistent on school rules when a class enters the room are less likely to face confrontation when the lesson begins, as they have already subtly signalled who is in control. Be calm but assertive when dealing with problems: going off at the deep end just provides entertainment for a class while raising your stress levels and taking its toll on your voice, not to mention the counterproductive effect of losing the students' respect and creating an atmosphere of loss of control.

Avoid getting drawn into the kinds of forays that some students like to set up. Insist that all questions are asked when you have finished speaking. It can be very draining trying to explain what needs to be done in the face of a flood of questions. Often the questions are genuine but the class have not yet learned to wait for an appropriate time to ask. Sometimes the questions are a deliberate ploy to stall you either for entertainment on the part of a few individuals or, in the case of classes with low confidence the questions are designed to delay getting on with any work. Keep your instructions relevant and ordered and close down any potentially diverting questions with a 'I'm not talking about that now' type rebuff.

Look after your voice

Use a quiet voice – it calms a class. It never ceases to amaze me that some teachers, having managed to get their class settled, will then bellow instructions with no regard as to the effect such volume has on the group. If a class is quiet, prolong the harmony by doing your best not to disturb it – whisper or talk with a lowered voice to individuals, write non-urgent reminders on the board rather than announcing them the second they come to mind. Most things can wait and if they can't, address the class in a hushed tone: 'Sorry to disturb you when you're all working so well but I need to just let you know ... thanks, carry on, you're working really well, we'll stop in about 10 minutes.' Do not let anything or anyone destroy this hard-earned and highly desirable tranquillity!

The voice is the primary tool we have as teachers and yet many of us neglect to look after it. Schools are hotbeds of infection and if you are feeling low it is very easy to catch anything going, so sleeping well, eating well and keeping hydrated is obvious but essential general well-being advice to follow.

It's easy to forget to stay hydrated during the day, particularly if you miss breaks because you are setting up for another lesson, dealing with students or you are simply too far away from the staffroom. Have a bottle of water with you and sip throughout the day. Keep it to hand on the desk, though if it's a sports cap ensure that it remains closed. It's amazing how many times a desk is shoved or a pupil trips, sending water over a stack of important paperwork. Boiled sweets are also a useful aid to keep your voice lubricated between lessons. If you've reached the state of needing throat sweets, keep your verbal output to an absolute minimum.

Curb your talking time

Keep it short
Keep your introductions short but long enough to explain adequately what students need to do. It can be tempting with rowdy classes to rattle through instructions at a pace fast enough to prevent interruptions, or to keep talking while you have the students' attention, wallowing in the peace and delaying the inevitable chaos that will reign once you utter the words 'Off you go!'. Other classes will keep you talking with flattering but distracting questions designed to reduce the time they spend working – over time this will weaken your voice.

Insist on silence
Never speak while someone else is speaking. Always insist on silence while you are talking. Allowing someone else to compete with you undermines your authority, and means that at some point you will have to go over what you have just said to the person who wasn't listening and anyone who was tuning into him or her, rather than paying attention to you. On top of that, it probably means that you have had to raise your voice slightly to be heard, causing further strain.

Write instructions on the board
This helps the visual learners in your group too. Write step-by-step instructions or numbered reminders either before the lesson starts, as you are explaining it, or, if turning your back on the

class to write seems to cause an air of disruption, as they are settling into the work. This means when a student forgets the instructions, you don't have to repeat them; you can simply gesture towards the list. Remember that many students do genuinely forget or get confused over what they have to do; having a point of reference will assist both them to get on and you to keep things running smoothly without constant vocal haranguing.

Get students to read aloud and explain

Share the voice load by getting students to take a turn in addressing the class. If you need to go over what has been done so far, or to remind a group of some previous learning, save your breath. Ask members of the class to explain what they remember or understand. This both involves and focuses the class. Similarly if work has been set which requires the reading of one or more texts as a whole group, seek volunteers to read aloud, or – if you need to keep certain characters on their toes – choose class members to read sections. Although reading a text well yourself is preferable to the sometimes painfully tedious reading around the class, selecting a couple of confident and eager readers ensures that everybody has read the text, and you have saved your voice.

Use gestures

Gestures are more usually associated with primary schools but are surprisingly effective at secondary. This method preserves the flow of a lesson and saves your voice. Many gestures are universally understood and often used subconsciously:

- fingers to lips representing silence
- raised eyebrows to signal surprise, usually that someone is not doing as is expected
- a shake of the head and perhaps wave of the hand to mean 'no' or 'not now'
- motioning with the hand downwards to show that all four legs of the chair should be on the floor
- the raising of the right hand to indicate that the class need to

stop and listen. Variants of 'look this way please' include pointing to the eyes and motioning towards yourself or the board and accompanied by a 'Melissa, this way please' or a gentle 'Andrew, focus', avoids needless torrents of whining about what the student is doing and should be doing thereby cutting out any potential for unwanted feedback by simply redirecting attention to where it needs to be.

Unnecessary answers

Steer clear of answering endless questions from the moment your students enter your classroom. Although the queries are often well-intentioned and innocent enough (granted that sometimes they aren't but are instead the beginning of a bit of supply-baiting!), it's best to reserve your energy and answer any crucial questions in a controlled manner when the class is settled. You are in a better position than the group to know which questions are crucial! Students don't realize how tiring it is to be bombarded with queries and concerns and are perfectly happy to ask 'What are we doing today' without thinking through the consequences of 20 others doing the same as they arrive at the classroom, or the fact that teachers seldom forget to explain to the class what they will be doing today. Think of it as a juvenile form of communicating with you and forgive them their enthusiasm – welcome it in fact – but usher them to their places with a polite 'I'll answer your question in a minute' or 'I'll tell you when you're all sitting down' or, if it's news or information a simple 'thank you', 'that's nice' or a smile and a nod should move them on their way. As a student teacher I was often alarmed when teachers appeared to ignore children's questions. I soon realized, after a spell of full-time teaching practice, that tactical ignoring is just one of the survival techniques that keeps teachers in school and not at home with a perpetual tonsil-pharyn-laryngitis cocktail. Be polite, but don't feel the need to attend to every enquiry made.

Checklist

- Choose your battles – some are worth winning, some are best left.
- Use your voice carefully.
- Use your voice sparingly.
- Use visual aids.
- Never talk over students.
- Stay hydrated.

Registration has never been a simple affair and is made all the more complicated for the supply teacher by the fact that every school seems to have a different system – paper registers, systems such as Bromcoms and computer registration. Some schools take registers in the morning and right at the end of the day, others after lunch or during every lesson. However, as registration is a legal requirement, it is essential that, if you have been requested to cover registration, you are fully informed of the how, what, where and when.

The recording systems prevalent in most schools today are a Simms-type paper registration (you mark students' presence on a pre-printed sheet which is then sent to the office to be scanned), or a computer registration (you log on to a laptop or the desktop in the classroom, locate the appropriate class register and fill in the appropriate code for each student). Some schools still favour the reliability of a traditional register (red circle, black slash) so it's always worth having black and red pens handy. Never presume that these will be available in the classroom – the teacher's desk may be locked or the pens may have gone 'walkabout'.

Assuming you haven't ended up taking registration in the solitary mobile classroom at the perimeter of the campus, nearby tutors are usually happy to answer any queries you have regarding registers. It is best to arrive at your room early enough to find out, if you need to know, rather than disturbing them during their register period, when they will be busy with students. Ahead of time, the best people to speak to for the low-down on registration are probably the office staff. They are the ones who cope with the idiosyncrasies of teachers and will be able to tell you whether the Simms sheet should be filled out in pencil or pen, or what code is needed to register a student who is late but arrived before registration has ended. As a rule of thumb, it is better to fill out Simms sheets with a pencil so that mistakes can easily be corrected. However, some schools insist on pen – in which case find out how mistakes can be corrected (usually with a simple vertical line through the error) before you reach for the correcting fluid! If there is any doubt, send a cover note to the office explaining. Should you be a technophile, whose blood turns cold at the sound of the Windows jingle, and have absolutely no confidence in your ability to wrestle with computer systems, it's probably best to play it safe and ask the office to provide paper copies of your classes for the day. They will usually be only too happy to oblige – providing you ask politely and strike the right note of panic – rather than risk vital data not being entered that they will then have to spend the rest of the day chasing up.

If a register doesn't arrive, the computer won't boot up or let you on and you can't get another member of staff nearby to log on temporarily for you, make sure that you create a paper copy of the register by writing down the first and last names of everyone present and send that to the office. If the group appear trustworthy you might explain the situation and either pass around a piece of paper or get a couple of students to write down names. Before the group leave, cast your eye over the list (to make sure there are no 'King Arthurs' or 'Britney Spearses' in the class) then perform a rapid head count and or read it out to check everyone's name has been recorded and that no one has added their mate, even though she has yet to show up, because they thought they saw her coming across the field ... Remember that the register is a legal requirement. In the event of a fire or even a student not turning up to school, the register is crucial in tracing them; if you have marked someone present on hearsay, the responsibility lies with you.

Find out who is responsible for picking up and returning the register. Many classes have monitors who collect and return registers from week to week but equally it might be you. Because secondary schools are so big it's worth picking up the register yourself if you happen to be going past the office. This saves having to try and find a 'volunteer' later if the monitor has forgotten, is absent or is reluctant. If you have been assigned both registration sessions with that particular group, it is a good idea, during the morning session, to clarify who will be responsible for bringing the register over in the afternoon. It's also best that students running such errands around the school are dispatched alone unless they are either very new Year 7s or taking money somewhere. In primary schools you will probably encounter the converse predicament – over-enthusiasm. You will no doubt ruffle feathers if you ask the wrong person to return the register – it is amazing just how good some memories are when it comes to recalling who is supposed to be responsible this week and that Adam took it back in the third week of September but that Macy still hasn't had a go.

The dinner register

The complexities of the attendance register pale into insignificance in comparison to the dinner register … be prepared! Schools with canteen-style dinner arrangements have dispensed with this cumbersome chore, but most primary schools will have some provision for collating dinner data and range from the simple hot dinner/sandwich affair to students having to select a specific meal. The most complicated system I have come across is one where there is a two-week set menu (so first of all you need to know whether you are on week one or week two); the students who are having hot dinners then have to choose which of the three options they would like (sounds simple enough but wait …); the three options are coded with both letters and colours and an appointed monitor is charged with the job of handing out appropriately coloured cards to fellow pupils that correspond to the meal selected, so that they can be handed in to the supervisors at lunchtime to avoid everyone suddenly deciding they want chilli even though they ordered cauliflower cheese. Finally the selections must be recorded by the teacher in the form of the letter code which isn't at all easy when the responses are either 'red please' or 'beef curry'! It takes little imagination to conjure up just how much potential for chaos there is in this for the unwitting supply teacher! Just be prepared – this is often a part of the day that regular staff forget is quite complicated and they are unlikely to go into as much detail as they will regarding other events and lesson plans. If the class sense you are not quite sure, their eagerness to 'help' you sort it all out can bring an otherwise calm situation to the point of turmoil, as everyone chips in with their version of how it all usually works.

Notes and notices

Another function of registration is the dispersal of information, sometimes in the form of messages which need to be read out and sometimes with letters that need to be handed out or collected in. Keep an eye out for lists that tutors may be keeping to check in any paperwork, particularly if that paperwork has to go directly to the office or another member of staff and will therefore not have been seen by the tutor. Mark off the names of students who have handed anything in, or make a note of it. Anything non-urgent should still be collected, though the temptation may be to ask the student to bring it in tomorrow – it may never be seen again otherwise. Put all paperwork handed in somewhere safe but obvious in the tutor folder. If there is no tutor folder because registration is conducted online, hand anything in to either the office or head of year with a brief note of explanation or leave the bundle in the tutor's pigeon hole (providing they are not on long-term absence). It's best not to leave anything on the desk where the common collective can access information that may be private or important communications which might stray in the general hustle and bustle of the day. Generally speaking primary teachers' desks are less vulnerable as there isn't the influx of various classes throughout the day, but all the same be aware of what you are leaving on the table. If a student brings in money or a cheque, send them directly to the office to pay it in.

If there are letters to give out, do so in an orderly manner! It is a good idea at primary – if you have the time – to read through the letter with the class and explain any implications. Then make sure that everyone puts their letter away in their bags or diaries, or whatever system the school may have for ensuring good parent/school communication. It's quite a good idea to do the same at secondary, particularly with the younger year groups, and if you have been given no activity to do in the time. Write the names of anyone absent on the remaining letters so that the teacher will know who to give them to when they return. Be cautious if there seem to be far fewer letters than students – they may only be for a certain year group (if the class is vertically grouped) or club. Some schools print enough letters per family so it may be that only the oldest in the family has to take a copy.

If you are really pushed for time, it may be better to delay giving out correspondence in a rushed and random manner and wait until the next day when you or the teacher can ensure that everyone has the right copy – check to see if the information is urgent first. Clearly a letter notifying parents of an impending bus strike or a first-come-first-served trip needs to go home as soon as possible, but other letters might be better handed out when there is time to ensure that everybody has a copy (and not just those who manage to grab one to stuff into a pocket on the way out to meet friends, leaving the returning teacher the task of working out who did and didn't take a letter).

Choose wisely when and how to distribute any paperwork. Asking someone to do so as you read out the register will focus attention away from you, causing more disruption. Some letters – the looming trip to Alton Towers or Comic Relief Day – can trigger the kind of excitement that may well be detrimental to getting the attention of the class for the 10-minute activity you've been asked to conduct. Newsletters, on the other hand, might be a useful five-minute silent reading session – in which case make your expectations clear, get the class settled and then do any quiet jobs that need doing such as signing planners.

Reading out notices can be a friendly opportunity to chat with the class on a less formal level, or it can be a completely galling experience when faced with a totally uninterested group who are clearly used to just chatting throughout registration and take it as an affront if you attempt to interrupt their social time. At primary, messages are usually very straightforward and, as you are with the class you are either going to be working with for the day or have spent the day working with, it shouldn't be too difficult to gain their attention.

Secondary classes, on the other hand, can be a completely different kettle of fish. They tend to fall into two categories: those who are generally used to some kind of routine and order and those who clearly are not used to a structured registration and have little interest in getting to grips with your style of leading in the 15 minutes they have to be there. You need to be realistic –

this might be the only 15 minutes they see you all week (if ever again) and you are of no significance to many of them. Once you have got the attention of the class, let them know that you just need to do the register and read out a couple of messages and then they can finish talking but it MUST be quiet or silent to call the register. Sometimes you can slip in the messages before you call the register, if not straight after.

Be selective – what information is vital for that day? Are there any messages for certain students that you can deal with individually? Secondary schools often push out huge lists of notices that may have no relevance to your tutor group and there's little point in you reading meeting times and dates for the trip to Wales if no one in your class is going. Writing on the board is a useful voice-saver. With one particularly rowdy group, I wrote up the room changes for the day, then insisted that everybody copied down those significant to them in their planners. I then wandered around the room, chivvying along groups and individuals in a non-confrontational but determined manner rather than trying to read out a whole list with people talking and then negotiating the shouts of 'What?' or 'Where did you say science class B is?'. Over the two weeks I had them there was a slow but gradual improvement in getting and retaining their attention for more than a couple of minutes – any improvement is a measure of success.

Behaviour during registration

In primary schools, the issue of behaviour does not tend to manifest exclusively in registration, principally because you are with the same class all day. In secondary however, standards of behaviour are often more difficult to enforce as time is very short and students quite often see this time as their own time. So, matters such as sitting on a chair, not eating or taking off coats are regarded as rules that do not necessarily apply. Not being a lesson as such, registration time can often lack a sense of purpose, although some very organized teachers develop daily routines which engender a sense of structure.

Registration groups are essentially pastoral so the atmosphere tends to be less formal and the order established in the class very often revolves around a relationship between teacher and class that has been nurtured over time. Your expectations of behaviour should be the same as in any lesson; remember that you may well be teaching members of this group or their friends, and first impressions and reputations count. There is frequently important information that needs to be dealt with so cooperation is essential. Reprimand and refer any problems but by the same token, once the admin has been settled, if there are no specified activities, take advantage of the relaxed atmosphere to either run one of your own activities or get to know more of the students or learn more about the school through informal chats.

Registration activities

All kinds of activities run during registration time – signing planners, silent reading, sharing, quizzes, problem-solving, but rarely are any plans left for this time at secondary level. Once you have got to know a school, you will get an idea of what kinds of tasks you could usefully bring to the situation. Where possible it's best to stick with the programme. Students will be accustomed to the routine and will generally settle more easily than if you introduce something new. Tutor groups seem to vary from teacher to teacher and this is one area where, unlike the curriculum, there is a little more leeway. To this end you will come across classes who are allowed to sit and talk and others that are so highly organized – not only will there be a checklist of what activities are carried out on which days either on the front of the register folder, planners or noticeboard – the class will probably come in and immediately get started.

It is best to keep the group gainfully employed. Individuals who have suddenly found their routine disrupted are more likely to lapse into racing around the room or shouting over to friends or 'remembering' that they have to see somebody about something somewhere (usually far away from the classroom), so even if you don't know what the group usually do, have something to fill 15 minutes. Games should be simple and pretty much recognizable to save long explanations only to be interrupted by the bell when you've just got started. Signing planners, often on a Monday is something you can do to maintain consistency and further establish yourself as a 'real' part of the school. Ask students to open their books to the relevant page (usually last week) – even if they haven't been signed – then move around the classroom while the group are engaged in an activity and sign them. It shouldn't take more than two or three minutes. I initial planners that haven't been signed and sign in full those that have – that way tutors can still sign if they have time and wish to and will know whose book had been signed on time, and parents can feel happy that the school is honouring its half of the monitoring deal. If anyone doesn't have or refuses to show you their planner simply make a note and pass it on to the head of year if you deem it necessary rather than let it become a big issue or a forum for your authority to be challenged. Heads of department in very efficient schools with few behaviour problems are often keen to keep on top of such tasks, others might be snowed down with more serious issues so make your call as appropriate.

Primary classes also will have activities. On certain days there may be assemblies. Other than that literacy and numeracy starters are popular, particularly as pupils take differing amounts of time to come in and get themselves organized. Having a task that they can come in and get on with is ideal. This is one of the times in the day where monitoring jobs come to light – the cleaning of the guinea pig, tidying the bookshelves, feeding live locusts to the Lilly the Leopard Gecko. Remember that it is your classroom for the day and that you can decide which jobs need to be attended to. If arguments are breaking out about whose turn it is to do what, or – even worse – locusts are breaking out of their margarine tub home as seven pairs of hands scramble to undertake said duty, it's best to say no to everyone and sort it out later. Lilly can probably manage until lunchtime today if needs be – your priority is to get your class calm and settled.

Assemblies

Assemblies are usually a straightforward affair and quite often a nice break as someone else takes charge! At primary, the two main responsibilities are remembering when the assembly is – as this can vary from day to day – and keeping an eye on the behaviour of the class during the assembly. Time flies by when you're having fun and adjusting to new or different routines and it is easy for literacy to run over or to forget that on Wednesday's Year 5 have an assembly before break. Therefore it is a good idea, if you are prone to such memory lapses, to put into place devices to remind you, especially if there are plenaries to run and a classroom to tidy before lining up to set off for the hall. Some class members are very good at clock-watching and might be employed to remind you, or a nearby member of staff might be willing to let you know when they are preparing to go. Failing that, set an alarm on your telephone or watch. Before leaving for assembly ask the pupils to remind you how everybody behaves during assembly (entering silently, looking to the front and listening, etc.) and explain that you will be looking for pupils being particularly good. At some schools, break promptly follows so it may be that your class will be expected to take with them coats, snacks and money rather than returning to the classroom – double-check the procedure in the morning.

At secondary, the main issues are actually being able to register your group and remaining informed of when and where. Times of assemblies tend to be more obvious (usually first thing in the morning) but year groups and locations can vary widely. In smaller schools year groups may be clustered together; in large schools year groups may be further divided into house groups. Find out who has assemblies when and whether classes meet at the classroom or in the hall or line up to be registered in the playground. Again variations are numerous and being prepared is the key to not being caught out. Hiking to the other end of the school to register a Year 9 group when they are assembled in the hall just a stone's throw away from the staff room is both inefficient and annoying! Schools that use electronic registers may rely on tutors to fill out a paper register on assembly days, which is relatively simple if you are able to recognize students but pretty much impossible for a supply teacher. This might be overcome if the class is expected to register in lines outside the hall, perhaps standing in alphabetical order but if students just file into their allotted rows and teachers record during the assembly then that presents problems. Another member of staff may be willing to help you out but failing that ask the person leading the assembly to request that your class stay behind at the end. The other difficulty presented at secondary is needing to be in two places at the same time – for instance, if an assembly runs on and you are due to be teaching elsewhere. The rule of thumb here is that your priority is the lesson. If you are teaching the same year group you are in assembly with then obviously there is no problem, you will all start late, but if you are due to be teaching Year 11 French and the Year 10 assembly is running late then let a colleague know and make a discreet exit. Somebody else can oversee your registration group but there may be no one available to settle and sort your Year 11 linguists.

Checklist

- ⁻ Registration is a legal requirement.
- ⁻ Have to hand a red and black pen, pencil with rubber and Post-It notes.
- ⁻ Have usernames and passwords ahead of time and keep them safe.
- ⁻ Avoid causing disruptions during register such as giving out letters.
- ⁻ Use settling activities such as silent reading to create the right atmosphere.
- ⁻ Only register students you have seen and send a note with the register if in doubt.
- ⁻ Find out about the system for recording dinner options.
- ⁻ Make a note of anything handed in (who and what).
- ⁻ Give out letters in an orderly manner and note the names of absent students on the remaining letters.

- Ensure that important and relevant information is relayed to the class.
- Have the same expectations of behaviour during registration as for any lesson.
- Have a 15-minute activity up your sleeve.
- Don't allow regular jobs and routines to hinder registration – your priority is to get your class settled and ready to learn.

Assembly

- Find out the who, when and where of assemblies. Ask! In the endeavour to get lessons covered simple routines such as assemblies get overlooked.
- Remind pupils of your expectations of both arriving at and behaving in assembly.
- Check to see whether there are any special procedures such as taking coats, sitting in alphabetical order, bringing merit slips, lining up outside to register.
- Be aware, ahead of time, where you are expected to be next.
- Let somebody know if, for any reason, you have not been able to accurately register your group.

On the whole, work left for classes is usually done with the supply teacher in mind and where possible, lessons are planned to be as painless as possible, be that setting enjoyable and not overly challenging activities for students or, in some cases even removing particularly disruptive students. To this end, notoriously 'lively' classes often find themselves with a DVD to watch or in the ICT suite, or, in primary, a very structured day is organized, packed with established routines and procedures in order that the group aren't too taxed by an overload of new activities and unfamiliar situations.

In some circumstances, staff know well ahead of time that they are going to be out of school and are able to arrange cover thoroughly, sometimes even prepping students beforehand so that – in the best-case scenario – your role is merely one of support and guidance as the group feel a sense of responsibility to progress or finish their work, knowing that they will be personally accountable to the teacher directly for their progress; some teachers definitely have the knack of being able to exert influence and high expectation from afar!

Often however, absences due to illness or emergency mean that planning lessons and resources are much more difficult, if not impossible to coordinate. Options open to the teacher are to stick to the lessons as planned anyway (though that may require specialist knowledge), dig out some relevant textbook or worksheet materials that will be relatively easy for any given teacher to deliver and for students to pick up or, in more extreme cases leave the organization to a colleague or head of department. Where a member of staff has been absent for a length of time all sense of continuity, and sometimes relevance, has often been abandoned in favour of a series of more 'workable' one-offs. There are of course occasions where for reasons seemingly beyond anyone's control, nothing is at all is left which can be a blessing or a curse depending on your outlook and preparedness.

Providing structure

You may feel completely at home with the area of the curriculum that you are covering or you may feel all at sea: either way your job is to look in control! By providing a structure for the class, you take ownership of the lesson regardless of whether or not you are an expert in that field. You are an expert in the field of teaching and you can present a framework from which your students can work. This encourages students to see the big picture (where the lesson is going) for themselves and allows them to take on board your expectations and the notion that they are accountable. With a clear structure, the class are more likely to stay on-task and you will be able to help them monitor their progress easily and noise levels will be much simpler to regulate. Getting the group to 'buy into the deal' by agreeing on what is manageable in the time allocated, and what rewards will be offered (from your list of options, not their dream treats!) definitely helps in motivating a group, though the bottom line (and starting line) is that the terms and conditions are ultimately yours.

If the subject or, in the case of primary, the year group, is familiar to you there should be little bother in delivering the lesson, behaviour allowing. If, on the other hand you're a science specialist now handling history or an English expert getting your mind around maths, or you're more familiar with Year 5 than five-year-olds you are going to have to rely on common sense and possibly the pupils themselves to provide insight. Treating students as the experts is often a very powerful ploy and, contrary to all those instincts that tell you are appearing vulnerable, will earn you respect so long as you run the show. The secret is to make the lesson your own.

Introducing yourself

We tend to think that students should just deal with whatever school life dishes out to them, to accept change as and when it happens and trust that it's for the best and on the whole they do;

but as adults we are much more able to see and understand the bigger picture and often forget that from a student perspective school can be quite an unstable environment with routines regularly disrupted and often without warning. So when Mrs Dyehouse's class see you sitting in their classroom or Mr DeSousa's French class are greeted by your rather anglicized 'Bienvenue!', allow them a little time to adjust.

In the bewilderment of the first few minutes, it is easy to forget to introduce ourselves. Imagine if you turned up to work every day to be greeted by a new boss, with a different set of rules and procedures that you need to learn about and come to terms with who didn't always make the time or effort to at least find out your name ... oh, yes, you do! Well, exactly – it can be confusing and disconcerting. And just as we would want to test the ground, feel safe in the hands of this boss, feel confident that s/he's up to the job and will do their best to look after our interests, so do your students.

So remember to tell the class your name. If you think that you might be so tied up with getting the starter underway as the group arrive and don't want to repeat yourself 30 times, write it on the board then introduce yourself formally when you address the class as a whole. If you are going to be with the class all day, let them know a little bit about yourself. If you specialize in the subject you've been landed with at secondary, or have some experience in it, let the class know. It's reassuring to feel a confidence in the stranger that has just announced she is going to be taking your GCSE chemistry class. If you don't have direct knowledge you are still an expert in teaching who has the experience to help this group get the best out of this lesson.

Try to keep the balance of firm but friendly: your class want to trust that you can handle them, and they will do their best to test you. Remember that it's no fun being shouted at by some stranger ranting and raving, so greet the group as you would like to be greeted and start with clear and fair expectations.

Many teachers take their own list of rules into school. You can do this on an overhead, memory stick, or laminated poster that can be placed on the wall.

Routine

Stick with as many of the regular teacher's routines as possible, especially at primary where routines are quite well ingrained. Always attempt to teach the lessons left, even if they do seem a little patchy. You might well prefer to switch to your own tried and tested ideas but remember that the class has a curriculum to follow; if it is distorted every time that their teacher is out, the continuity and understanding will really suffer. Only as a last resort should you revert to your emergency back-up plans. Although they may not be related to what they have been doing in class, your role in maintaining stability in behaviour and active engagement will be appreciated by all involved.

The start – setting the tone and expectation

Some classes are brilliant at giving the impression that they know what they're doing, and many even believe they do, but never just let a class get started with just a modicum of instruction unless you have seen them in action before and know them to be well-motivated and purposeful. Even with very trustworthy classes, it is as well to create a formal start if only to remind them of your expectations. Set the tone for the working atmosphere and agree what will be completed during the lesson. It is definitely the case that reasonably independent starts to sessions, with little formal input is not necessarily a good indicator of how the lesson will pan out. Without a shared vision of behaviour, or an agreed version of how activities should be finished, it might not be long before things start to get out of hand and you find yourself desperately trying to regain some form of control in what appeared to be a mature class.

Students of all ages much prefer to feel that you are in control and are more likely to resent your authority when you try to make demands later rather than earlier. With a formal start, you can establish not only what students are aiming to achieve by the end of the lesson but also get them to anticipate any problems or predict any resources they might need. This is the time to iron out any queries about the work set, either by sharing your own knowledge or asking the class to offer answers. Usually someone in the group will know but failing that, be honest that you're not sure; come to a collective agreement with the group to assume that, for example, section C must be asking you to describe your home town in French or that as no one has any idea how to work out the lowest common multiple we'll skip section two. When consulted, students are typically very mature and responsive and it wouldn't be surprising for them to agree to replace section two with another that they understand.

Outline how you expect the class to behave. If you have done all the discussion necessary and all that is required is to write up answers, there is no need for talk; and you can remind the class of that. Classes that are used to working in silence won't expect anything else. I have learned over the years that conceding to quiet chat in reality means that work doesn't get done; I prefer to have work completed then allow time to talk. If the lesson requires research or group work ensure that the group remains focused by building in set feedback times where students are made accountable for their progress. Double-check that everybody knows what they are doing; explain that you won't be answering questions once the group has started and that you don't want to find people flocking around you with questions the moment you've set the group off. Run briefly through the list of things to do again, explain to the class that you want see everybody working, remind them of any relevant rewards or sanctions and then set them off.

Anticipating problems before they arise

One of the many things we learn with experience is to anticipate problems before they even arise. It is very easy to get carried away on the enthusiasm of a class when they tell you that they're working on their plays in groups at various points around the school and you send them off only to find that the key people with the scripts are absent and you now have five groups around the place very considerately filling the time by playing their own games or chewing the fat because they can't do the play but have neglected to inform you of their dilemma.

A formal start to the lesson means that you can establish exactly who is doing what, where they will be (in the unlikely but not inconceivable situation that they have been working elsewhere), and what they will have achieved in the time given. I usually add a very specific target so that individuals are accountable – reading out what they've written, playing a piece that has been composed, acting in a performance, showing and reporting back on something they have been making. If it seems the class will need very rigid guidance, it is a good idea to have one, possibly two feedback sessions to ensure the class are staying on task. Without such planned pauses, some groups will fritter away the whole lesson doing other things. With short focused sessions students can see their peers are getting on and will be motivated to do something themselves. It also means that individuals or groups who are genuinely struggling will get an idea of what they are supposed to be doing and will be able to emulate, if not come up with something completely their own.

Setting goals

As a supply teacher, setting goals and guidelines is the best way to ensure progress is measurable in such a short time. They are particularly effective if the lesson you are teaching is followed by a break or lunchtime though rewards for achieving them also work well. Once a class associates you with being someone who expects targets to be met, they will more naturally focus on completing them. If you include the group in the negotiation of how much can be done and the rewards (or sanctions) on offer, so much the better.

Challenges

Keep the targets realistic but challenging; making them too easy will mean that students, realizing they can easily achieve it, will sit and chat. It's better for the target to be slightly more difficult as you can always praise and award points anyway for continual hard work. When students complain that they will never be able to complete the work set in time and panic that they will be punished because they're slow writers or 'not clever', I am always resolute in pointing out that I never keep people in if I can see that they've been working; if they haven't finished but they've been chatting then that's their responsibility but if they've been working throughout the lesson but haven't finished, I explain that it would be very unfair of me to keep them in and that I just wouldn't do that. This makes my expectations crystal clear and by and large does the trick both at primary and secondary level.

Timings

Once you have the class settled and listening and have read through the work that needs to be done, read through any questions or texts or have individuals explain to you what they intend to do as the next step of their project and make an assessment of how long each section should take. If there are questions to be answered, calculate roughly how long they should take to answer and connect that to a time – 'So that's seven questions in section A – that should take about 15 minutes, so everyone should be done by quarter to, ten to at the latest' – and write it on the board. This really sharpens focus: most students respond well to specific targets and if not personally, they will keep up because they don't wish to be the only person lagging behind. Surprisingly, this is the case even in tougher classes.

Targets can be set at all levels, whether it be a number of paragraphs to be written over a period of time at secondary, or a number of words or sentences at primary. Admittedly younger pupils are less likely to have such a developed sense of timing as older students (though this is debatable!) but will respond to gentle reminders 'five minutes to go' just as well. Electronic timers are freely available on the internet to download for those with computers and projectors available. Keeping the working time to short spells is good at all levels as it allows for intense spells of concentration followed by five or 10 minutes respite to share and either feel confident that they are on the right track or to be able to change tack before they veer off in completely the wrong direction.

Jot down agreed timings on the board:

Section A – 15 mins

Draw diagram – 5 mins

Write report – 3 paragraphs, 7 mins each paragraph

Feedback – 10 mins

Pack up – 5 mins

When you have structured the lesson with reasonable timings, it's only right that you should expect the work to be completed within time (no excuses).

Monitoring

Explain that you will be monitoring progress by stopping at a certain time and that people will read out the answers or their first paragraph or report back on their research or feed back on what they've done. If a break or lunchtime is imminent, set the minimum that you expect to be reasonably completed. Clarify that those who have not finished that work will not be leaving to go to break. You will need to carry through this threat but it's well worth the time to establish your reputation in the long run.

Offer bonus rewards for pupils completing beyond the minimum expected or completing everything. I usually have a three-tier system if enough work has been set: minimum amount to get you out of class on time; bonus points (smileys/stickers/low level rewards) for the next section; bigger reward for everything completed.

Personally I rarely treat with sweets but many supply teachers do and this might work for you. Many things work as incentives such as a spell on the internet, free time in the library or perhaps, for infants, a visit from Hamish the penguin who likes to sit on the table of groups who are working very hard. Where possible, incentives are better than sanctions but both have their place. See page 115 for more on rewards.

Keeping track

Planned breaks also allow for problems to be addressed either directly by you or other members of the class, or the participants themselves guided by some reflective questions from you. If a student claims that s/he couldn't think of anything to write, check if the individual picked up some ideas having listened to the work of others; if not, you need to agree some intervention either from yourself, a TA or even a fellow student. If a group has made little progress due to one or more of the team refusing to cooperate, discuss what can be done to get back on target. They may just agree to stop messing about or may ask to be split up. If they don't appear to making sensible choices, divide the group or move or swap pupils round. If a project has made little or no headway because some crucial work is missing, get the group to reflect on what can be done about the situation. In some cases they may concur that the best course of action is to start again; failing that ask them to come up with a different but similarly-styled assignment. Again, if having the choice causes too much conflict or is so limitless it's paralysing then step in and set something very specific.

Rewards and incentives

Incentives are a massive asset in your toolbox as a supply teacher. Sanctions such as being held back for a few minutes at break and lunchtime are certainly powerful and should not be shied away from, as are referrals to effective teachers in the school – but both are limited. Good incentives are not only a better bet but a more positive way to motivate students who will see you as a fun teacher delivering rewarding lessons rather than a battle for which they gear up.

Finding out what will motivate a class is best done with the class itself. Some staff reward with sweets. I prefer not to do this, as for me it gives the wrong signals and also conflicts with the health messages we are constantly trying to teach. Besides that I have seen students jump through hoops for sweets, then misbehave, turning what was a genuinely intentioned reward into a form of blackmail bribery. Try stickers and stamps, five-minute games and contrived privileges – sitting on chairs rather than the floor for storytime, being allowed to take your blazer off, listening to music (if school rules allow). It's all a question of perception: I very often market my plenaries as treats at secondary – so playing vocabulary tennis can be hyped up as 'packing up a little earlier and playing a game' if everyone has worked well. Being awarded points in a game is often enough of a reward in itself, the role of being the class' top scorer.

When offering incentives it is absolutely necessary to be unambiguous about what you are expecting. To earn the privilege of your table leaving for lunch first, or play Sevens or even the once-in-a-day-opportunity to tidy up the book corner, students need to be clear about what they need to do to qualify for such sparkling prizes. It may be working without talking for 20-minute spells, writing 200 words, remaining in their seat or putting up their hand not calling out – but it needs to be measurable and achievable.

The best way to get the behaviour that you want to see is to get the class themselves propose and agree on the criteria. They are mostly ruthlessly earnest and usually demand high standards of themselves. Keep targets attainable by keeping them short and clocking them up. It would be both unreasonable and unrealistic to expect a group to work in silence for long spells, but in short bursts with an opportunity to talk and sort out problems in between, means that the class could instead aim to chalk up three or four silent sessions.

7

LESSONS –
GETTING GOING
AND
MONITORING
PROGRESS

From the distribution of resources to the movement of students, there are some simple strategies which you can use to help the lesson progress smoothly and for you to check on progress.

Presentation of work

This is one element that always seems to go to pot when a regular teacher is away. Some students will of course dutifully underline work, write in and underline the date and title and use sub-headings, but many will take the opportunity of having 'not a proper teacher' to let standards slip – they won't bother with titles and will write in a funnelled channel down the middle of the page or just on every other page, and won't worry if the writing is actually legible. It's worth making a point about presentation at the beginning of the lesson. The class probably need reminding anyway and it is another subconscious signal about your standards. It is also a good way of monitoring work and providing opportunities for positive feedback.

You might remind them by double-checking the standard procedure. In many schools this is firmly glued to the wall or in the planner. Have a flick through a few books to get a feel for the usual standard of work and try to pitch the level there. In classes where time is not taken up just getting pupils on-task, it's good to insist on a certain standard of presentation. This keeps the group focused, indicates that you are looking for quality work and confirms that you are interested in what is coming in and not just baby-sitting. A group concentrating on getting the small things right is more likely to be settled and get the big things right too. It also means that you can dish out praise for a relatively easy-to-achieve goal, which helps to establish a positive atmosphere.

Reading through texts, going through questions

Although it is tempting to just write instructions on the board – 'Read pages 78–81, answer questions 1–9 using full sentences . . .' – it is always worth taking the time to read through texts and run through questions with the class. This allows you to establish what needs to be done and it means that you know everybody has read the texts and understood the questions and task before they start. This should constrain the amount of pandemonium that may ensue if not. Otherwise this will happen: those that can will whiz through the work completing it in 15 minutes but without answering in full sentences; then they will resent you for insisting that they rewrite the sentences in full; they will either refuse to do it or spend the rest of the time rewriting the questions whilst very loudly-under-their-breaths plotting your demise. If they do finish everything in the time you may be left scavenging around for something else for them to do, at the same time as trying to help or persuade others to get on. Meanwhile those that feel they can't do what has been set will waste time chatting (if you're lucky with the person next to them, if not to friends sitting across the room); when you question how they're getting on they will exclaim that they either don't know what to do, or don't know the answers and you'll end up spending time coaxing them towards the relevant section of the text, and working twice as hard just to get one or two students going. During this time, while you are racing around trying to get students on task, the tone of the classroom will have been reset to 'casual chat-time' and the rest of the group will have taken to nattering. In the worst-case scenario, even those students who are usually obliging when it comes to work will be off-task and your time will be deployed between trying to help those who will be adamant that they still don't know what to do (and put the blame your way by claiming that you won't help them) and cajoling those who understand what to do to get on with it.

By running through everything, setting goals and agreeing on how you intend to check progress at the beginning of the class, you can make sure everyone is clear and put the onus on the students to be responsible for their output.

Noise levels

Many supply teachers feel uncomfortable getting groups to work in silence. Personally I don't have a problem with silent working because it offers everybody the chance to really concentrate on what they are doing. Chatting quietly only really works when work needs to be discussed. Payback for silence can come in the form of five minutes' chat-time as a reward. If a group is used to working in such conditions they won't be either surprised or resentful if you apply the same expectations as their regular teacher. In fact, not doing so may engender an atmosphere of free-for-all! On the other hand, trying to get a group who are used to a much freer working environment will cause bitterness and a headache for you in trying to enforce it: select your tolerance level with this in mind.

Keep your focus on the work produced by using planned intervals to make students accountable and praise their progress. Short spells of work interspersed by feedback and consequent praise should help eliminate unproductive chatter. Chatter does tend to spread and alter the whole working atmosphere of a class, so try to keep on top of it by reiterating what work needs to be done. Never be afraid to try for silence; lots of students in your class will appreciate it even if they don't say so.

Use a laminated set of symbols to indicate the level of noise at which you expect the group to be working or what class rules should be followed. These are four main situations: listening to the teacher (hands up to speak); group discussion (taking it in turns to talk); working in silence; and working quietly with a partner (feel free to alter the categories to suit your regular circumstances). Run through your expectations with the class beforehand and display the code of conduct you expecting with a blob of Blu-Tack. If the class seems mature enough to discuss the symbols, ask them to predict what each symbol means – otherwise introduce them with your rules.

Moving around the room, distributing and lending equipment

Most lessons need equipment. As a basic you will be dealing with pens and paper, but textbooks, handouts, worksheets, glue and scissors are also standard staples. It's worth putting in that little bit of extra effort into the organizing of the distribution of materials to save yourself the aggravation of having to quell a full-scale riot later on. For example, placing a pile of books on a table at the front of the classroom and asking the class (effectively en-masse) to come and get their books will often result in a pile-up of students all converging on one spot in order to look for their book. It would take an extremely self-disciplined group to resist the temptation of pushing and shoving their way out or into the hub at the front, or lobbing books overhead to peers at the back. Similar instances of congestion can be engineered when primary pupils all try to collect items from their trays simultaneously. As a Year 6 pupil, I remember a lovely new teacher inviting us all to come and sit in the book corner at the same time; the ensuing stampede resulted in the 'walls' of the area (low bookcases with thoughtfully placed plants and ornaments) crashing to the floor, soil and fragments of pottery randomly strewn.

Keep control by moving small groups or individuals at a time; tables or rows or named students moving, or collecting then returning before the next group are allowed to go. This is a useful method for getting groups into and out of a classroom too, and works well at all levels. However, judge carefully with older secondary groups: assess their entrance before trying to organize them in a manner that they will find patronising. The chances are they'll be so reluctant to have to move at all that any necessity to do so will involve a few getting up and the majority chiming 'Oi! Get one for me will yer ...?'.

As a rule of thumb, unless you are teaching a very practical subject, it's as well to encourage students to stay in their places. Where possible have one or two students distribute materials, or even do so yourself if it seems appropriate – sometimes handing out items is a great excuse for a stroll round and chat with pupils in all areas of the classroom (especially the back!), just to reinforce your presence and interest. This is an ideal opportunity to check uniform, jewellery and that mobile phones are away and no one is chewing. I regularly carry the bin to the chewer as it saves the fuss of a protracted journey to the front (where the bin is usually situated) socializing on the way and often executing a dummy throw anyway.

At the same time quickly monitor progress and remind individuals of what you're hoping they'll have completed by the end of the session, or simply learn some names and discover something about them – what lesson they've come from, whether they're having a good day, are they happy they know what to do, etc.

Another way to distribute books is to have them on a table close to the door; students collect theirs as they enter. Groups often arrive in dribs and drabs and this is one way to make the steady trickle work to your advantage. Have something for them to do, even if it's only to rule off the last piece of work and write the date and title that are on the board. Obviously this is only possible if you are there (and are able to locate work and books) first but it is an efficient way to meet and greet on a personal level, get to know names and calm or remove unacceptable behaviour before it infiltrates and spreads. With textbooks, which can be quite cumbersome, ask two or three sensible types to give them out.

Depending on how calm the lesson has been, collecting books back in can be conducted in a variety of ways. If there is a staggered finish to the work, it might be possible to ask individuals to bring their books to you, or to a specified table as and when they're ready. Make sure that you are there to monitor the returns – the prime spot to double-check that the work has actually been done to your specification – or you will end up with a random stack of books splayed across the table and probably onto the floor. Failing that, get a student at the front to ensure that all books are facing the right way up and in a tidy pile. If the class are ending the exercise together – perhaps you've run a plenary based on the work done – it might be as well to take a more systematic approach. Books can be collected in by volunteers or, students specified by you, from table groups or rows. Alternatively books can be handed to the end of rows or collated in the middle of tables to be gathered by one or two students. In rows, movement can be restricted further by the ends of the row then passing their books forward.

It might sound excessively authoritarian and these lengths probably won't be necessary but I have come across classes where just a couple of people out of place are enough to disrupt an otherwise reasonable atmosphere. With these systems of collection it is best to insist that everyone then returns to their seats and sits down before you let the class go. This means that you can ensure that everything has been collected to your satisfaction and visually sweep the classroom, checking all desks and the floor are clear.

Sometimes, books and worksheets mysteriously don't get handed in, either because tasks haven't been completed or, more frequently with older students, because it's simply too much of an effort to move from their places. A quick way to check is to either count the number passed in or, even more effectively, allow students to go when you've called their names. Once you start reading aloud names from the books handed in (I usually start from the bottom of the pile so that those who have followed requests quickly are not inconvenienced) an assortment of others are guaranteed to suddenly come flurrying in. Be careful that this is done in an orderly way though – read the name and watch them go, individually or in groups of three or four, and then read out the next group. If you simply read the names continuously, those that haven't handed in their books will take the opportunity to escape during the bedlam of chairs being scraped and farewells being shrieked!

Keeping a record of borrowing

Items that have been borrowed have a habit of not being returned, particularly pens! There are various ways of keeping track of what has been lent out but I find the easiest way is just to use a corner (preferably one out of reach of passers by who might casually erase your lists) of the whiteboard to record who has borrowed what. Either list names and what has been borrowed or write names under sub-headings such as 'pens'. With some of the more compliant classes, I ask the student to write their name on the board when they come up to the front to collect the item, or after I have delivered it to them, depending on how much is going out, or ask first student to write names of subsequent borrowers. Otherwise I write the names, but sometimes there's enough to be attending to without individually asking students their names and how to spell them. If there is a danger of false names being logged, then just make a note on your seating plan. At the end of the lesson either ask the individuals to make sure that they personally bring the items to you during the packing-up time and ask them to rub off their name once you've checked it (which they love doing!) or do it yourself if lists are likely to just disappear.

Alternatively have all borrowed equipment returned before the class begin to clear up, at the point where you have the attention of the whole group. It all really depends on just how much has been borrowed. With resources that most of the class need, perhaps highlighters or scissors, it is easier to give one to everybody or one per table, whether or not they need it – many students have their own highlighters. This makes it easy to collect in without discussions of whether you gave a highlighter in the first place: 28 out, 28 in is so much less complicated.

Planned breaks also allow more specific monitoring. They are a good indicator of how quickly the class is progressing through the work. If they are making good progress you can reward them and throw in another couple of challenges. If many seem to be struggling you can acknowledge the difficulty and their effort and amend the assignment accordingly. If a few have very obviously not done what was expected, realizing that their peers have is usually a good enough reason to buck up. Again, acknowledge what they have done; praise good work or good progress and get them to state what they are going to have done by the next feedback session. There is little point in admonishing what hasn't been done at this point: instead keep them focused on what you want from them. The embarrassment (whatever they say) of falling behind their peers is usually enough to spur most students on.

Checklist

- Take control of the lesson by creating a structure for the students to follow.
- Start by introducing yourself.
- Try to stick to as many regular routines as you can to keep the class more settled.
- Insist on a formal start to the lesson where you can establish exactly what needs to be done and run through expectations of behaviour.
- Try to anticipate problems before they arise so that you can deal with them before they cause disruption.
- Set goals and agree on timings to help keep pupils focused.
- Monitor progress and problems with feedback time.
- Offer incentives and rewards to motivate.
- Maintain standards by drawing attention to the standard of presentation you are looking for.
- Go through texts and questions to ensure everybody understands, rather than run into problems later on.
- Don't be afraid to have the group work in silence if it suits the activity.
- Move students around the room in groups if the class seem excitable.
- Consider carefully how to distribute and collect in materials.
- Keep a record of items borrowed and make sure they are returned.

8

LESSONS -
OBSTACLES

No matter how well a lesson appears to have been planned there are a whole host of obstacles that can hold up or disrupt your teaching.

'We've already done this!'

'We've already done this!' is a plaintive cry known only too well to supply staff and sure to cause alarm as you realize you are going to have to think on your feet in order to avoid the class collapsing into chaos. Sometimes the class actually have already done the work which may have been set by a colleague who is not familiar with the group: they may have done something very similar or they may have glanced quickly at the title and decided that they've already done the work without looking to see that it is in fact a completely different activity within a topic. They may have learned through experience with other supply teachers that, by claiming to have already done the task set, they don't have to do something they don't 'fancy' doing; or they may have learned that this will delay starting work while the supply teacher scrabbles around in a panic trying to find an alternative lesson.

In the first instance, respond don't react. Take the time to establish the facts before racing off in a flap. It is easy to fly into a panic, particularly if the group seem lively, particularly earnest or likely to revolt if they are not immediately set to something productive. Get everybody's attention by insisting that everything is put down, students stop talking and turn to face you. Insist on silence and then orchestrate the investigation by allowing pupils to put their case, one at a time, so that you can build a clearer picture of what is going on. Seek evidence in the form of work already in books. Ascertain whether the work was set by the teacher they now have or in another year group or another teacher. You might ask the group to tell you how they went about tackling the project last time. In this way you can make a professional judgement as to whether to go ahead and stick with the work, amend it, seek a new assignment from another member of staff or come up with something of your own.

If the work the group claim to have done was done a long time ago, or they seem vague about their answers, acknowledge their anxiety but explain that you're going to stick with it anyway. Justify your reasoning by pointing out that it's what Mrs Dowie has specifically asked them to do, or that it sounds slightly different from the other work they are describing, or both. Reflect on the advantage of them already being familiar with the subject which should make the assignment that much easier. In other words – 'It won't take you long then!' Be honest in pointing out that by the time you have tracked down other work, there won't be much of the lesson left and that on balance it would be better to just crack on with this. Acknowledge their apprehension and sympathize with their situation but firmly assert that you've decided it's to be done anyway and that you will leave Mrs Dowie a note expressing concerns on their behalf. Then get on with it!

If, on the other hand, there is evidence that the work has been done relatively recently (and this does happen!) you have the choice of: seeking the advice of another teacher, either by popping next door – if the class seem trustworthy; sending a note to a nearby colleague; or cobbling together something yourself. If you choose, or are obliged to, sort it out alone, you can either stick to the theme by perhaps choosing another activity from the book they are working from, or amending the current one, so that it has a different slant. Failing that, you could start from scratch and put into action one of the one-off lessons you have tucked up your sleeve. By all means seek suggestions from the class (they are often very good at providing genuine compromises) but do so in a controlled way: allow them to take it turns to put forward a proposal and be absolutely clear with the class that ultimately it's your decision and you won't be argued with. Sometimes not wholly-useful suggestions can trigger ideas but if not, they will have bought you some time to think of a plan B. Explain why you have decided to do what you're planning to do and thank the class for their ideas and patience; then inform them of the replacement activity; set the structure, the targets and rewards as you would normally.

Everybody getting stuck

There will inevitably a lesson or two where no matter how well you seem to have run through the activities, pupils will all get stuck at the same time or one question will pose difficulties across the class; you might find yourself chasing round the classroom assisting individuals or pairs in explaining what to do. Meanwhile the rest of the class, having given up on you ever getting there to attend to their personal needs, will have kicked back and be catching up on the latest gossip, hiding a pencil case or applying copious amounts of make-up. If you get to the point where you feel you are doing more work than the class collectively, it is time to call a halt to the proceedings and take charge from the front again. Insist that everybody stops, puts everything down and pays attention to you, even those who do know what to do – they may be useful in sharing answers. Then go through the particular question again, if necessary writing ideas on the board, perhaps even modelling an answer. If it's the whole exercise that is causing difficulties, try to ascertain what the problem is (understanding the question, finding the answer, presenting the answer) and give guidance – model or get the class to cobble together an answer between them. If the whole thing is too difficult and you are unable to provide direction, you might choose to switch to a different activity or skip the difficult bit. This is a very rare instance, as teachers tend to leave under-challenging rather than over-challenging tasks but if it should happen, just leave a note explaining the changes.

'It's in my locker!'

Avoid sending individuals on long searches for work. Generally if they have it, they know exactly where it is ('in my friend's bag', 'in my locker') and it should be no more than a two-minute collection exercise. Anything more vague ('I handed it in I think', 'Sir saw it', 'it *could* be in my locker') – give up and find a plan to do without the work, perhaps sharing or photocopying someone else's.

Requests for the toilet

Requests to go to the toilet are an awkward but unavoidable matter for supply teachers to deal with in school. At one of my schools the headteacher's preference was that students simply excused themselves as we would expect any adult to do. Once the novelty of the freedom had worn off, the students felt respected and didn't tend to abuse the system. In other schools, perhaps because property has been damaged or items taken, there is a policy of nobody out of the classroom during lessons, in which case the answer is quite straightforward.

When I was training I learned a tip from a teacher that has stood me in good stead when I'm not sure if the need is genuine, particularly with younger children. He said 'Say: ''Ask me again in 5 minutes'', and if they're desperate they'll be back before the 5 minutes, and if they were just bored they'll forget.' I sometimes try a bit of negotiation such as 'When you've finished . . .', in an attempt to divert attention. Sometimes I open with a plain old 'No' or 'Not at the moment' and again, if they're really desperate, they'll soon be back. It can be very difficult to resist those painfully strained faces though, and let's face it we don't want to actually stop anyone who really needs to go to the toilet, just all the others who fancy a break now they've seen a couple of their friends go.

At secondary, it's more usual to say no, but at primary it's a difficult call, especially when you imagine young Ben in wet trousers and his mother marching up to the school to complain that the supply teacher wouldn't let him go and how would s/he like to be stopped from going? I once had a class of Year 3s who suddenly seemed to inundate me with polite requests and once I'd exhausted my delaying strategies with the first two or three, it seemed difficult to justify saying no to the rest who had worked pretty well and completed their tasks. It was impossible to determine the genuinely cross-legged from the impostors. As a deterrent to those just out for a little stroll round the grounds, I explained that they could go but I would be noting down who requested to go and giving my list to the teacher when she returned which seemed to quell the flow (as it were!). Not being quite so familiar with the bladder control of Year 3s, I elected to let their regular teacher discuss the sudden epidemic with them when she resumed office after lunch. If I am teaching a class before break or lunchtime I will often offer to swap the time taken with time out of their break. Pupils really desperate to go will happily agree, whereas social wanderers either change their mind, or at the very least get back extremely quickly.

Find out the practice in the school from another member of staff and where possible stick with it. Make your opening gambit a 'No', followed, if pushed, with a delay, perhaps a conditional release ('When you've finished all the questions/up to number 7'); keep a record of who was out when and for how long, just in case something does go asunder during that time and you're called to account for any absentees.

Dealing with disruption

Always insist on silence when addressing a class. It's more difficult to set up the expectation to begin with but it's worth it in the end – classes will get into the habit of listening when asked. If it seems a bit draconian, and it can feel like that at first, to both you and them, override that thought and bear in mind that if the class see you as someone who doesn't mind a bit of background chatter, the struggle to get attention will become harder over time. Allowing talking signals an acceptance and students become incensed when you later appear to change the rules.

Ways of first getting attention vary from teacher to teacher, and depend on personality and mood, class and atmosphere. I have three main lines of approach: very reasonable, appealing to the group like adults (which works very well in primary schools); humorous, smiling and joking but also being firm; and the 'I'm not in the mood for this, get yourself sorted, quickly!' tactic, usually adopted when there seems to be a lot of fuss and attempts to be reasonable have been generally disregarded. I am quite open with classes in telling them that yes, I am fussy and I do expect pens to be down and faces to be turned my way and silence when I've asked for attention; I demonstrate this by stopping if someone picks up a pen. I'm sure it's what they are all thinking anyway so it may as well be confirmed! So, this is the blank canvas, let the disruption begin ...

Disruption can take many forms, an endless stream of messengers at the door sometimes, but more often within the class. It either stems from one or two personalities in the group, a group within the class or – in some extreme cases – a whole class, usually a class that has had such little guidance they have become law unto themselves and even the students who would usually be sensible elsewhere have reached the stage of joining in.

Never be offended by what students say and do; the trick is to not let things be personalized. Whether at primary or secondary, students are still children trying out new, or sometimes, very well-established strategies and patterns of behaviour. If you can view tempers, sulks and strops with distance and humour and encourage and positively acknowledge every new attempt to start afresh, then you can't go too far wrong. That's not to say that poor behaviour should be accepted; indeed it should always have a clear consequence and the students should know that you will always take action to ensure that your teaching and the learning of others is not disrupted. Grudges should never be held and every new encounter is a chance to get it right – think *Groundhog Day*.

Interpreting and devising seating plans

If your potential troublemakers haven't already identified themselves on their entrance into the classroom (in the various ways they do), cast an eye over the seating plan, which often highlights the hot seats. Look out for anyone seated alone, blocked to the wall or on the desk adjoining yours.

Although you are only there for the short haul, rearranging seating plans can still be beneficial. It may be that different students act up for you than their regular teacher and you need to respond accordingly. Where possible it's best to stick to the original plan, if one has been left, as this is the system that the class are familiar with and changes to the norm often stimulate further disruption. However, if things are not going well, feel at liberty to make your own changes; moving students may stir up resentment but importantly it puts you in charge of the classroom.

My general tactic to minimize disruption is to interrupt or block lines of sight between lively individuals. It is a skill that improves with experience but don't expect miracles. Redistributing pockets of chaos doesn't always work immediately – it just helps to manage the overall situation in the first instance and sometimes it just provides a challenge for those determined to cause a disturbance.

Where to move students to is another practical problem. Sometimes spare seats are available and sometimes you will have to rearrange others. It's a bit like a game of chess; like the parts of a chess set, your students will have set moves and the test is to uncover their motivations and engage a suitable game plan.

Rows and columns

The swiveller

Some students need the constant reassurance of their peers when they are acting up. Without nods, giggles and smirks on tap they soon lose confidence. The supporters range between those who want to be in with this personality and those who fall into line and acknowledge them to avoid being singled out for being a 'keeno' or whatever the local term is. Ardent fans will go out of their way to champion the disrupter by laughing and joining in, refusing any requests from you to turn round or ignore him/her, usually because they are so desperate to keep in with that person. Probably the only way to break this cycle is to remove at least one of the party from the room. The incidental co-conspirators (the ones who smile or snigger but look a bit nervous about it) can be taken out of the equation by relocating the heckler to another position in the classroom.

85

At the front in the middle

Because these students depend on support, cutting down their ability to survey the classroom can severely curtail their ability to command such a large audience. From the sides it is reasonably easy to view pretty much all of the group in one gaze, particularly if they are at the front. With a slight swivel, in the guise of twisting to see the board, head propped up on hand, this student can gain as much attention from the group as you can with little more than a rove of the eye. A move to the front in the middle will ensure that any turning has to be a deliberate move and one that you can pick up on. It also restricts the surveillance to only 50 per cent less of the class without a lot more effort. Being in the front line means that you can stand in close proximity to the student, able to establish meaningful eye contact or tap on his/her table if s/he turns around, without having to interrupt your teaching.

For fervent 'swivellers', those who just genuinely can't seem to help themselves, help might be at hand with a move to the back. The back of the class is a little unorthodox in terms of classroom control, classically where troublemakers head as soon as they enter the room, but it holds some largely untapped benefits. To begin with, because it is not a position in the classroom associated with being reprimanded, the guilty party will often not feel as humiliated and move with relative ease. By moving distractions to the back, you can relieve the reluctant incidental collaborators by getting them out of the visual firing line. Now, to actually reinforce disturbances, they will have to turn around; getting them back on side is comparatively straightforward. If they do turn around a simple 'Kev, this way please', should bring them back into line. The only way that the disturber can gain attention then is to call out inappropriate comments or actually yell out names in which case if s/he refuses to stop, s/he must be removed from the room.

Boxed in

Persistent socializers are another common form of disturbance though more usually during working sections of the lesson, as opposed to when you are addressing the group. These are the students who are not so concerned with screeching across the classroom or seeking attention, and have no particular malice towards you, but they see lessons as a time to catch up on the gossip; they will be both offended and mystified should you suggest otherwise. The best way to temper these devoted chatterboxes is to confine their lines of communication. It is can be better, in some cases, to move their reluctant victims (usually friends who don't have the heart to ask them to be quiet) than the actual natterer. That said, a strategic move to one side of the classroom where they can be boxed in with three or more of those wonderfully inert students who stick to the programme regardless of interruption (should you have three available!), is worth a try.

Blocking them in breaks their line of vision both horizontally and vertically and, as they are at or near the front, they will have to turn completely round to chat. This will be immediately obvious to you, in which case you can just remind them with a quick 'Work please Rachel'. Rather than pleading with the chatterer not to talk, appeal to those surrounding them to ignore them – 'David, do me a favour and ignore Nicola, she needs to get on and talking is just getting her to trouble, thanks'. After a spell of frustrated attempts to communicate, Nicola will usually settle down. Should they attempt to communicate beyond the box, just place yourself in their line of view, almost coinciden-tally – you don't need to say anything unless they look up at you when you can quietly interject 'Come on Justin, stick with it'. Gesture to them that they need to turn back and continue with their work. If they are particularly eager to talk, you can, in ideal conditions, reinforce the box with other sensible students. The next step is more likely to move them to another classroom; the threat of that might be enough.

Three in a row

The three stooges appear from time to time in classes of all ages and abilities, with interjections and banter that can be difficult to contain. One ploy is to split them up and spread them across the classroom, endeavouring to break all lines of engagement – vertical, horizontal and diagonal. Admittedly, this is easier said than done and can lead to a situation where you have simply increased the extent of the disturbance. A nifty solution I came across recently, from a fellow supply colleague, is to seat the miscreants at the side, one behind the other. While not guaranteed to eliminate the fuss completely (but which strategy is?), placing the trio one behind the other makes it more difficult for them to trigger off each other without the effort of turning around, at least for two in front. If you stand at the back of the column of tables, anyone turning around will immediately be visible and a quick 'Face the front Caroline' should minimize the repartee. By being at the back they will never know whether or not you are watching and when they sneakily turn to catch a glimpse of whether you are, you can immediately leap in – 'Josh, focus'; they will usually instinctively turn back.

Your position

It's a good idea to move about the classroom as much as possible. Clearly if you are doing board work you will be leading from the front but there are plenty of opportunities to lead from the back too. Being at the back not only means that you have the whole class in view and the class don't know whether or not you are watching them, unless they turn round, before embarking on some crime or misdemeanour. If you already have written on the board everything necessary – your name and today's tasks – there's no reason you can't lead from behind. You may have a student scribing instead or student-led feedback from the front. This is my favourite spot and I often place my 'live wires' there with a table to themselves so that I can sit behind them should they need guidance with the work or help in concentrating. Played with lightness, it is a friendly but assertive strategy. If a student should look to me, I smile and discreetly offer help – 'You okay? Need any help?' More often than not the student politely declines and get back to work.

If students are particularly sensitive to me sitting next to them, I monitor from just behind either left or right shoulder, about a metre away. Avoid staring over shoulders as this is not designed to be a process of intimidation, but look elsewhere. I usually move a chair and calmly sit down there so that potential disruptions are diminished. I always focus elsewhere, perhaps even idly reading through a student's planner or spare textbook, silently signalling with a circling motion of my finger to any 'ogglers' to turn around and get on with their work. Just being conscious of my presence is often enough to keep the status quo in check. If the pupils you are monitoring repeatedly insist on checking to see if you are still there, peel yourself away from the book or other distraction, and greet them with a smile and either an offer of help, or, if they've actually been working a 'Well done, you getting on alright, need some help?'

If it doesn't have the desired effect of suppressing chatter, the next best thing is to offer help immediately or provide a stream of constant but very hushed reminders that the students need to keep focused. Every time they begin to talk, cut in very quietly (whisper if the rest of the class are working in silence) with a redirection – 'Susan, work please', 'Susan, no talking', 'Susan, keep with it', pleasantly but assertively. Your continuous but gentle interruptions will eventually break the desire to chat – chatting will prove too much like hard work! Field any little excuses for talking:

> *'I was just asking her about question 7.'*
> *'I'll help, what do you need?'*
> *'I just wanted to borrow some Tippex.'*
> *'Just cross it out, that will be fine.'*
> *'I just wanted to borrow her rubber'*
> *'Okay then.'* – let her do so, there's no need to be unreasonable!
> and, as soon as she's writing again –
> *'Well done.'*
> Avoid being drawn into any innocent conversations, calculated to divert such *as*
> *'Miss do you live near here?'*
> *'Carry on with your work.'*
> *'I was only asking.'*
> *'Yes but it's time for working now.'*

Keeping doggedly focused will work eventually. Always praise the right response and an occasional quiet 'Well done' or 'That's great' to an individual or the rest of the class should keep them on track.

This approach is a little like getting restless children off to sleep – you hang around so long that in the end they pretend to go to sleep just to get rid of you, and in doing so, fall asleep. Here they pretend to be concentrating, with the occasional sideways glance at a friend – then find that they are ironically becoming quite involved in the work.

Disruptive students are often the ones who are trying to cover up the fact that they believe they can't do the work. Sitting next to a student who seems to be making a fuss will determine whether s/he needs extra help. If the student doesn't, the chances are she or he will just on with work to encourage you to move on. However, if the student is struggling you can discreetly offer support without causing embarrassment in front of the class. Support by pointing the student in the right direction and follow up with plenty of tactful praise.

If the students in question persist in complaining that they don't want me there or can't work with me so close, I always promise to go just as soon as I feel confident that they are settled and working; when they have worked for five minutes uninterrupted I do move, leaving the chair in place as a reminder and just in case attention spans flag and I should need to pop back later.

Warn students about their behaviour before moving them, unless it is very obviously unacceptable; then ask them to move to a specific seat, changing other students if necessary. If an individual refuses to move, you have two options: you can either carry on teaching, a chance for the student to change the behaviour, in which case you've got what you wanted anyway; or ask the student to step outside. If you do speak to a student outside the classroom, establish very quickly what the problem was, acknowledge any grievances. Tell the student that you would still like him/her to sit where you have asked, explaining, if necessary, that this means s/he won't be disturbed by another student whom s/he has probably just blamed for the incident.

Thank the student for his or her cooperation and allow the individual back in. If the student continues to refuse to move, s/he needs to be permanently removed for the lesson.

Group seating

Primary classrooms (and an increasing number of secondary) are organized into grouped tables, which tend to have a much less institutional feel. If not ability-grouped, pupils will have been arranged into combinations of individuals who work well together; it is best to insist that usual places are taken. The same principles of blocking or removing lines of sight between pupils who have an inclination to disrupt still apply. When you are addressing a class for a length of time, seat them around you (usually on the floor is easier, though Year 6 often are granted the privilege of moving their chairs – manage this by moving one group at a time) or turn their chairs to face you. Pupils who have to twist around to see you for longer than a minute will be uncomfortable and easily distracted.

Sitting in a spare place on a table group or next to/near to a pupil causing disruption, usually has the effect of settling both the pupil in question and the rest of the class. Onlookers will be keen that you don't sit by them! If the pupil is struggling, a little discreet help and praise is more likely to glean positive results than constant urging to get on.

Motivating groups to work quietly is much more practical (that's not to imply that it's necessarily easier!) as inventive and novelty incentives are usually greeted with enthusiasm. Tables can compete to be the first to line up, or to have 10 minutes in the book corner, or to choose the book for you to read to the class.

Mobile phones

With many schools forbidding them, mobile phones are yet another distraction for teachers to deal with. In spite of bans, subversive texting, taking photos and even taking calls in class are everyday occurrences in some schools. For the supply teacher, preventing their use can be a nightmare. In schools where you find the appearance of phones recurrent, it might be an idea to remind students informally as they enter the room (if they are handling phones on their way in) or formally request that phones are turned off or turned to silent at the beginning of the lesson, alongside a warning of what will happen to phones that go off or are out.

My standard line is that if they do go off or are out of bags or pockets, I will have them until the end of the lesson; if there is any argument they will go to another member of staff (specify who) until the end of the week. When the class start to protest of the unfairness of this (which they do!), I point out, in my nicest, jolliest, 'way-I'd-like-to-be-asked' manner, that none of the sanctions will be necessary anyway if phones are turned off, which usually is enough. However I only do this in schools where I feel confident of being backed up.

It's probably best to try to avoid all confrontations over mobile phones. Students will be very reluctant to hand them over and if they are willing to, you then have the responsibility of keeping them safe. Placing them on a desk or even in a drawer leaves them open to the danger of being picked up either by the owner or an opportunist. Tucking them away into a pocket or bag could lead to you leaving school having forgotten to return the items. The best course of action is to just keep insisting that phones are switched off and put away. If there is a recurrent issue with a number of students continuing to text or even call from the phones during a lesson, then call for assistance; clearly it is disrupting the lesson and breaking school rules, and refusing to do as you've asked should be enough reason to seek back up.

MP3s and iPods also appear regularly in secondary lessons. Most schools don't allow personal music in lessons but check the general line. I mostly refuse to allow them and take the same policy that I have adopted for mobile phones, but if the students are being allowed to use them in other lessons then it is very difficult to justify. With particularly difficult groups or students who seem to be more settled with music it might be prudent allow music for the overall sake of the lesson – if work is actually being done you might decide that this is a positive trade off. When you are addressing the class however, insist that all earphones are out. If you offer the use of music as a privilege for working well, and on the proviso that they're only to be used during working time, then allowing the use of personal music players may work to your advantage. Be aware however that senior staff may have a different view and may drop by and challenge students, thereby putting you in an awkward position. Seek advice from a well-respected member of staff about what is generally acceptable and take it from there.

Passing notes

The old fashioned version of the text message! If passing notes causes disruption, remove them with minimal fuss. Fold or keep them folded and put them straight into the bin. Reading them aloud may cause undeserved embarrassment for a member of the class and will certainly stir unhelpful excitement. Putting them on the desk means they are still in reach of anyone determined to either retrieve or steal a look. Most students will draw the line at foraging through the bin but if you suspect they might, tear the note up. Secreting the note away into a pocket may cause concern with the student who has written the note that you are going to read it or possibly pass it on to another member of staff, resulting in diverting concentration from work. The note may be about you and reading it may cause offence, embarrassment and an obligation to take action. Best binned, preferably without a noticeable hindrance to your classroom patter.

Free time

It's a mistake that we've all made at some point in our careers offering free time. There is no such thing as 'free' time in a classroom – it is a misnomer! Classes can be very convincing when urging and pleading with you to grant them time to do whatever they want, in a manner that can certainly imply that they are capable of being mature and well behaved in exchange for a bit of free rein. The truth is that any time unplanned and unregulated in a class is almost certain to cause you more stress than you bargained for if the time in question is longer than five minutes and the students are other than sixth formers who are too laid back to cause a stir. It's not that students intentionally cause trouble given such a liberty, their intentions are genuine: it's just that when it comes to it, free time just never delivers what it seems to promise.

The thought of doing no work is what primarily appeals but the reality of what fills the space is always disappointing. It usually starts off okay, perhaps with a few activities that the class think they'd like to do or even just a bit of time to gossip. It always seems to get out of hand as students tire of the activity and decide a chase around the class would be more fun; or a little teenage flirting is indulged in, in the form of whacking each other with rulers, bags or anything else that comes to hand. Then you find yourself expending more energy than you would running a lesson trying to hush the group and redirect individuals to do, well what exactly? Then there's the fear that if the group become much louder, the teacher next door or passing senior management will be pop in to see what all the noise is about.

My advice is to never offer free time, even if you have been left stranded without lesson plans. Apart from the fact that it is not a legitimate activity in school – imagine the class has had a series of supply teachers all agreeing to not having to work – it is very difficult to organize for even the best-behaved groups. It starts off with groups agreeing that they would like to chat quietly or draw or devise a play or occupy themselves with a game of hangman on the whiteboard (there is ALWAYS a group that want to draw on the whiteboard!) and within 10 minutes the artists have concluded that they can't draw and have decided to make aeroplanes instead, the actors can't agree on who should be which character, the hangman-ers have run out of words and the chatters are excitedly yelling gossip across the room.

No, the best course of action is to do a Henry Ford and offer a choice of colours so long as it's black! Ideally have one activity up your sleeve ready to wow them with. More than one can be offered, if you prefer to give the illusion of choice and democracy, by facilitating a class vote (in secret if needs be: eyes closed hands up anyone peeping gets has their vote voided) but bear in mind that with a vote there will always be disgruntled punters who didn't get their way and will grumble in spite of the fact that they are getting out of 'work'.

Electrical equipment

DVDs, video recorders and televisions are all capable of delivering a blow to even the most smoothly planned lessons – never trust them! There are occasions when you actually can just switch on the power, press play and watch the exact section needed for the lesson. There are many more when the lead won't reach the socket without having to demolish the classroom to manoeuvre the TV into place, the cable connecting the DVD to the TV has disappeared or become disconnected, or the DVD is missing or damaged. Where possible always check and have a run through beforehand; it saves trying to resolve the problem while your class marauds. If you are not technically minded and there is no technician in sight, there are usually a handful of enthusiastic experts nearby who will be only too happy to guide you in setting the equipment up. If not, use the time to seek out or devise an alternative lesson plan.

Checklist

- Take the time to listen to a class but remember the ultimate decision-making comes from you.
- Don't be afraid to stop the whole class if lots of small groups of confused students threaten to break the working atmosphere – take charge.
- Avoid sending students on searches for work – it is rarely found.

95

- Where provided, follow the teacher's seating plan; if necessary make your own strategic moves.
- Deal with mobile phones and note-passing swiftly and without fuss.
- Avoid 'free' time: it usually ends up being much more difficult to manage.
- Check electrical equipment works before having to cope with it in front of a restless class.

9

LESSONS -
MARKING WORK

As a supply teacher you are expected, where possible, to mark work. This is sometimes easier said than done, especially when you have a day racing from department to department or punctuated by students being withdrawn to see the nurse or practise for the school concert or have photographs taken. Sometimes you may be granted some 'free' time which could be used for following up work. Your reputation (and therefore likelihood of being invited back), will be greatly enhanced if you are able to leave a pile of marked work ready for the returning teacher – there is nothing worse than having to come back to a heap of marking. Teachers returning to a consignment of unmarked work are unlikely to make it a priority, particularly if the work is deemed to be not strictly relevant or of a much lower standard than the group are usually capable of. In turn, work left unmarked obviously devalues any work done with a supply teacher in the students' eyes. Therefore, in the long term, your job becomes more difficult as students don't see the point of putting in any effort into work that won't be acknowledged. Furthermore, marking in the class with students rewards them with direct feedback; consequently they regard their time with you as useful and relevant rather than just time-filling. Indeed, in some cases classes may not have had a permanent teacher in months – and their behaviour will probably reflect their disaffection – in this instance, marking will be even more valuable as the students desperately need to feel that their time and effort at school is reciprocated in some form.

The easiest marking consists of simple question-and-answer exercises – answers are very specific and can be marked en-masse. Having agreed on a time that the class will go through the work, call them to attention; the students swap books with a neighbour or use a different coloured pen or pencil to the one they've been using and check through their own or peer's work. I usually carry a class set of red pens, invaluable for both marking and independent editing.

Even if there is no precise mark scheme for the work, make one up; students are really motivated by points and will be more attentive in their eagerness to clarify how many points they have gained for different sections of a question. I sometimes add in points for spelling or punctuation, though it's worth warning them beforehand. So, if an answer happens to be a name there might be one point for the name (or one each for first and surname) and a point if it has been written with a capital letter – this way you can get into the game of totting up points. If you haven't been left the answers, you can probably work them out, or at the very least verify the correct answers as offered by individuals in the class. If there is disagreement, go with the consensus; if there is no consensus leave the question out and move on. Don't pretend to know anything you don't know; express your considered opinion but admit you don't know for sure. Where difficult words or answers in another language have been required, ask students come up and write the answers on the board so that the whole class can see the answer and correct spelling mistakes if necessary. Students usually love coming up to write on the board and this can help to fill out the time if necessary. I always encourage groups to be honest with their marking, explaining that as teachers we need to see what has been learned and what we need to revisit. I ask students to put a single line through their incorrect answer and write the correct one next to it. You may well find individuals either scrawling in answers they originally got wrong or didn't do at all but it's not probably not worth making an issue of it at this point unless it was meant to be a test; either discreetly remind them to use their marking pen to make changes or just happen to go and stand near the offenders as you are going through the answers – this usually does the trick.

For more complicated answers (perhaps full sentence, inter-pretive or opinions where the gist of idea has to be explained) have two or three examples read out and then clarify what you're looking for. Some students may ask you to verify their answers personally but if this becomes a bit cumbersome get them to take some responsibility by saying 'What do you think?', then nodding or praising them for making the right assessment. For written pieces, where students have been asked perhaps to research and write up or create a piece of writing, aim for everyone read out at least a couple of sentences or their 'best' paragraph. If a class lacks confidence, reward them for just reading out their work and find something to praise – good ideas, nice use of words, a lovely phrase – also acknowledge quality work with higher ability pupils but keep them on their toes by directing them to what you want to hear rather than letting them choose their best section (they can do this too if you have time). Where I know students are able but could be a touch more conscientious I will stop the class periodically and ask them to read what they've written, for instance for section two, the first three sentences of their third paragraph, or the very last line of the first paragraph. For anything read out, I ask students to put a tick in the margin and 'read aloud' so that your verbal marking is acknowledged.

At the end of the marking session, students total their marks and write them in their books. You might like to pick a handful of random students, or even all, to tell you their scores so that they can get an idea of how well they did. Try to end on a high note, even if the scores are low by rationalizing them – 'That wasn't bad for a first time', 'There were some difficult questions there', 'I just think of what you could have scored if you'd finished' or home in on what they've learned by getting them wrong – 'So Carly, what's the French word for bread ... well done you've remembered now'. Even if they haven't behaved perfectly during this lesson, now they know that you are going to follow things through. They will be happier to focus next time so long as they don't feel that this session hasn't been about making them feel stupid.

Reading aloud

Coaxing 'volunteers' to read can be quite a skill and does improve with time but is not always foolproof. With most classes there will be one or two enthusiastic individuals who will quite happily do all the reading aloud but that defeats the point of making accountable and keeping a handle on the less willing participants. It is useful to have a class list but picking someone who refuses to read early on might put you in a position of a stand-off – which unless you are incredibly persuasive you will lose, entailing a minor mutiny as a whole load of others take a vow of silence. With an incredibly shy class give team points and praise just for reading and develop the relationship from there. You might allow friends to read out work on behalf of reticent or diffident students or even read aloud work yourself. Either way, when it has been delivered, always praise the students and get them to write 'read aloud' next to the section they have read with a tick and a corresponding reward if appropriate (primary pupils love to copy a funny cartoon face you have drawn on the board) so that their effort and your monitoring is recognized.

Projects

For ongoing projects, perhaps research or work of a more practical nature, use a reflective plenary to double up as feedback, monitoring and marking. Ask the class to jot down the following either as a series of bullet points or a thought-share diagram:

- What they have done today
- Whether there were any problems and how they tackled them (successfully or unsuccessfully)
- A list of the steps they need to take next.

Give the group five minutes or so to reflect on their performances; then have them report back to the class one at a time, either in a circle or as selected by you. If you have time to go through and tick their summaries and make a brief comment such as 'good work', 'smart thinking', 'great ideas' or 'well tackled'. It takes minutes but will reinforce that you are actually taking an interest in their work and they will remember that next time you visit.

Making time

Praise and reward effort and reflection as well as top marks. Leave enough time to award credits or merits if you have promised them, as this may require signing planners. You will have to have a system ready to be able to put your signature on 30-odd journals while still keeping the group diverted from a general melee. It's a good idea to have planners open to the credits page in preparation; this sets the tone to a positive start and makes it easier to award credits as you go around the class. Write some criteria on the board beforehand so that students can copy in a statement (rather than you repeatedly writing it) which you can then nip round and sign. Have behaviour, effort and achievement comments such as 'working quietly', 'completing all questions', 'choosing eight excellent words', 'reading aloud' – so that the class know what you are looking for: the power of suggestion should never be underrated!

Finally, collect in their books or work done on paper, unless the class need the books for homework or revision – ask a reliable member of the class and if in doubt, let them keep them. Ideally collect the books open to the page of work they've done so that you can add any comments if you have time, or so that the returning teacher can easily see that the work has been completed.

Comments

Time permitting, and it shouldn't take long, it is definitely worth whizzing through the books just to add a comment. Comments don't have to be terribly detailed or insightful – great if you are able to pick up on what has been done well or even set a target – but just an acknowledgment to the student that you have seen his or her book will be valued. Build up a stock set of phrases as you go through to aid your speed and keep your remarks positive. Remember that you are a relative stranger and as such may not yet be welcomed as a critical friend; aim instead to build up an encouraging, working relationship.

If you are marking work after the lesson, add formative marking and types of comments or targets regarding

- working well/attitude
- presentation

- correct work
- quick target – good word choice, good sentence beginnings.

Checklist

- Marking is part of the supply teacher's job.
- Where possible, instant feedback is preferable.
- Reading aloud is a good way to monitor – record that you have done so by awarding a credit and writing 'read aloud' in books.
- Use plenaries to encourage pupils to reflect on their progress. You can always remark on this if you don't feel qualified to comment on the standard of work.
- Make time to reward pupils with smileys, credits or stickers.
- A brief comment in books will acknowledge the students' effort and indicate to them that you have an interest in their work – a great longer-term motivator.

10

CLASSROOM
MANAGEMENT

Behavioural issues are one of the biggest concerns for teachers in schools these days and are probably one of the main reasons for teachers leaving the profession. It could well be that the teacher you are covering is absent due to stress and you may be taking one or more of the classes that have contributed to his/her stress. Unless you are either very lucky, or have been able to get yourself on the supply list at a couple of very select local schools, chances are that you are going to encounter some pretty 'lively' classes, some of which will have seen so many supply staff that they are not only completely disillusioned with the education system but are by now past masters at running circles round any new face.

Schools vary widely in how they follow up behavioural issues. At some, support for supply staff is excellent and systems for follow-up so thorough that just a warning is enough to settle students back to work. In one school I've worked at heads of year run daily lunchtime 'detentions' where any problems can be immediately pursued and supply staff are made to feel just as important as permanent staff.

At others, the process for dealing with discipline matters is a little less well defined. Heads of department or colleagues can be called upon providing they are not at that point handling their own demanding classes. 'Time out' or its equivalent (a room or area in the school where students work if they are unable or not allowed to work in their classes) is an option so long as the person in charge of the room isn't absent or called away to a meeting and that senior management are actually available, and not too snowed under with other requests to get to you on time.

I don't wish to paint an overly bleak picture but a realistic one – difficult situations are much easier to handle if you are at least mentally prepared and not taken completely by surprise.

Confidence

One thing you must ooze as a supply teacher is confidence. It's a must for all successful teachers but especially important for supply staff who have to make a convincing impression in just a short amount of time. Planning and tips undoubtedly help but the most useful tool you can have in your arsenal is the ability to appear in control.

I asked Scarlett, a Year 10 student, what advice she thought I should offer to supply teachers, the conversation that followed went something like:

Me: *'What advice should I give to supply teachers?'*

Scarlett: *'Er, try not to cry.'*

Me: *'Really? Have you or your class made a supply teacher cry?'*

Scarlett: *'Yes one ran out, everyone was talking and no one would listen to her at all. Then another teacher comes into to help them but as soon as they've gone everyone messes around again.'*

Me: *'Can you tell whether you'll be able to get away with things?'*

Scarlett: *'Yes!'*

Me: *'What as soon as they walk in?'*

Scarlett: *'Yes!'*

Me: *'What should you do when you walk in?'*

Scarlett: *'Be confident, like when they come in be ''Hi class, this is what we're doing today'', not just going straight to the desk and being quiet and shy.'*

Me: *'What about sending people out if they're rude or naughty? Does that work?'*

Scarlett: *'Yes sending people out is scary.'*

It's always really interesting to tap into the views of students. If you ever get a moment to, students really are the experts when it comes to what makes a good teacher.

Confidence comes with time and experience (and, unfortunately sometimes ebbs with time and negative experience) but, to a certain extent, can be engineered.

Try to view yourself from the point of view of the students

- Do you come across as friendly but firm?
- Do you come across as someone who doesn't really want to be there?

- How do you respond to incidents of rudeness or refusing to do what you've asked?
- Will the class regard you as being overly authoritarian or weak?

The line between being reasonable and a soft touch is sometimes a very fine and tricky one to judge.

- Show confidence by walking tall.
- Look students in the eye, projecting your voice – that doesn't necessarily mean being loud but speaking with conviction.
- Speak at a commanding pace and with conviction and don't be afraid to pause. Rattling through instructions in the space you've been granted, before the chaos descends is not a good sign!
- Wait until your audience are all ready. If your lesson is being followed by a break or a lunchtime, explain that you will wait until everybody is quiet and if that means that the lesson runs over then so be it.
- Look around the class – sometimes raising your eyebrows at a student doing something they shouldn't be will be enough.
- Give your instruction then move your eyes so you are not staring directly at the student – doing so will often prompt a response and usually not the one you were hoping for! 'Pen down please …' or even just a 'No thank you' followed by shifting your gaze is usually enough.
- For tougher classes, reiterate exactly what you're looking for, using positive language and very clear directions: 'I want to see everybody with their pens down, looking this way and listening' or 'No talking, this way please'.
- Keep the instructions simple and unambiguous – this makes it easier to pick off those refusing to follow instructions.

If there are one or two not doing as asked, follow up with a polite but firm insistence directed at them personally – 'This way please', 'Pen down' or 'Listening'. If they are persistent or even rude when you remind them, let them know that if you have to speak to them again that there will be a consequence: you'll pass their name onto the head of year/deputy head (or whoever it is that wields the power; or you'll be having two minutes of their breaktime; or ask them to step outside. Depending on the behaviour of the rest of the class, you can either have a quick word with the offender at that point or leave him or her outside for a few minutes until you have spoken briefly to the group.

Without the support of the group, a few minutes' isolation should be enough for the individual to calm down and then to be keen to go back in so keep your reprimand short and positive, focusing on what you would like to see – 'You in your place, listening when I'm talking and completing the work okay?' – then follow up with a quick reminder of the choices you feel you have if that person continues to disturb the class from learning or you from teaching – 'Otherwise I'll have no choice but to call time out/ ask Mr Reeves to have you/pass your name to Mrs Steele, etc. If the group is fizzing, concentrate on getting them started and then deal with your miscreant. Don't waste time and energy dragging up the incident and ranting about again. If the student stood outside and you have been able to get the rest of the group started then you have achieved what you needed to; focus now on explaining the task, describing what you want to see and reminding of the consequences of those expectations not being met (and be prepared to follow them up).

If a group of people is holding you up, either suggest a whole-class sanction – 'I can see this whole group not leaving on time/ coming back at lunchtime', or record the names of those causing the hold-up either on the board or on paper (less public). The whole-class sanction is less popular generally as it isn't fair on those who have done as asked and you run the risk of those who have been cooperative deciding that they may as well be hung for a sheep as a lamb and joining in. On the other hand it is difficult as a supply teacher to get to grips with names and faces quickly and easy to get confused as to who has said what. There are also often powerful influences in the class who will bring their influence to bear on those messing about if they think that they are likely to be punished as a result.

Having a sanction that can be worked off seems to be the most successful. I mark up the number of minutes that a class has kept me waiting and promise to have the time back – classes who know me, know I will. When the class has settled and I have their attention, I explain that the time can be earned back by listening to instructions and working, not talking. When the class displays the appropriate behaviour, I cross off the minutes on the board one at a time. I try to cross off one early on and then take the remaining time in the lesson to cross off the rest. This is always accompanied by quiet praise and words of encourage-ment to keep going. If the behaviour reverts to calling out, I chalk up another minute. If the disturbances are very obviously from a few names, I sometimes write on the board the names of the people who are working well and will be leaving on time. This reinforces for them that they are doing the right thing. At this point someone always chirps up that their name isn't on the board but should be, to which I reply that I can't put the names of people calling out and that I want to see them getting on with their work. Again, anyone persistently disturbing the working atmosphere can be removed.

Tone and pace

In teaching, how we use our voice is crucial to the response we gain. Although they probably wouldn't analyse it as such, pupils of all ages can determine your confidence intuitively by homing in on the clues your voice emanates. Any combination of wavering tones, faltering speech patterns, awkward hesitations, talking too quickly or perhaps with a little more volume than is necessary, will signal a crisis of confidence and therefore open up the floodgates to further stages of testing.

Appearing confident to begin with is part experience, part preparation and part charade! At least that's the way it can feel. Be aware of how to effectively vary your voice to its best advantage. Be conscious of how you speak. Notice how other staff use their voices and to what effect. Adapt your tone and delivery to suit your situation. Generally a measured pace and with a clear and deliberate delivery is the most captivating combination, using calculated pauses to retain attention. Pauses possess great power – they create great anticipation. I discovered this quite by accident as a student teacher when I completely forgot what I was saying one day mid-rabbit. I found the class hanging on my every moment of silence like they never had to my usual enthusiastic rapid-fire tirade. Students who had clearly being doing other things stopped and looked up sheepishly, suddenly paying attention because they had misread an expectation in my muted interlude.

On the other hand a lethargic class can be 'yakked' into action by a bout of animated haranguing. It denies them the chance to chill out and turn off or the space to chat with a neighbour ...

'Right then let's go, pens, pencils, planners out, Jude yellow books to everyone please, Felix one textbook each, date, title underlined, starter on the board, pen Harvey, let's have that bag away quickly Poppy, facing this way Richard, ruler, thank you, George, why are you still talking ...' This stream of instructions, jollying the group along as you wend your way around the classroom requires the group to listen and act quickly; it engenders a sense of urgency and purpose but would be as effective as whistling in the wind with a group gabbling at a similar pace and noise level. A better a strategy to bring a loud, busy class down to the speed you want, is to adopt a quiet, calm intentionally slower pace.

Primary teachers are much more likely to make use of intonation as a tool to attract attention and emphasize interest, surprise, excitement or express grave disappointment. This exaggerated manner not only directs the pupils' responses but clearly indicates who is in charge. Secondary students, and even older primary pupils are more likely to find this technique condescending however, if overdone.

Novelty voices also work well in gaining and attaining attention at primary level. Anyone who has ever read a story using an array of voices and accents will have witnessed just how enraptured their audience become. Combined with puppets or toys you are sure to gain immediate interest. Although I could never imagine doing it, a very outgoing and melodic early years colleague I know actually sings instructions in order to get the class on board – it really works!

Repetition is an invaluable communication device in both primary and secondary. It comes naturally to most experienced teachers who realize the value of crystal clear instructions from the outset to save yourself the trouble later of explaining again to those who have only picked up fragments of the original instructions. It works because it provides a more efficient way of receiving and processing information. This information is not only completely new to students but also competes with the internal dialogue that pervades all our minds at any one time. It also by supplies a structure that helps recall information later and places emphasis on crucial steps (such as writing names on work!) – 'So you need to collect your book, and a sheet with the diagram from Liam okay? So, book, sheet, then date, title and copy and label the diagram. When you've finished that collect an orange book from this desk here and copy the diagram on page 57 alright? So, book, sheet from Liam, date, title and then what Rowan ... good, what page Hanni ... great, off you go!' It can feel like over-egging the pudding, but in practice explaining only once, even though it seems simple, often just results in confusion further down the line ... so, repetition, repetition, repetition!

Finally, never underestimate the power of positive language. Use language to direct the class to the behaviour you want to see; use praise to acknowledge the behaviour you wish to encourage; and use your attention to focus students on what needs to be done rather than want you don't want.

Sending students out

Sometimes the behaviour of some students makes it impossible to teach. If one or two individuals are preventing the lesson from moving forward it may be necessary to remove them from the room either temporarily, this allows you time to get the rest of the class settled and started, or permanently if their behaviour has been so unacceptable and warnings have had little or no effect. There are no hard and fast guidelines for such a procedure.

It all depends on the nature of the class, the expectations of the school and the behaviour of the student, the combined elements of which will steer your professional judgement.

At a couple of the schools I work at, one primary, one secondary, I send out any student entering the room in a loud and unreasonable manner straight away and warn them politely but firmly of the consequences if their manner does not improve with immediate effect. This sets the tone for both that student and the rest of the class and, on the whole, deters any further bother. At another school I would be hard pushed to pick out the individuals as that is the general method for entering a room: my priority here is to settle the group, gain their attention – starting off with a conflict will only promote further hostility.

At both primary and secondary, it is as well to follow a staged approach.

1) Swiftly and tactfully remind students to listen (without too much focus on the individual so you avoid inviting a retaliation which the student might feel obliged to respond with in the presence of peers).
2) Warn more explicitly – 'Adam, I can't teach while you're talking you need to listen please' perhaps followed up with an 'if I ask you again you'll need to go out.'
3) Ask the student in question to wait briefly outside so that you can reason with him or her away from their peers. Here, the student chooses whether to come back in and work, or to be removed to 'time out' or another class or to follow the procedure at that school.

Of course it is never that simple! There may be one or more offenders. Some teachers are very good at diffusing the situation with a little humour in order to get the class on side and save the need for anyone to step out. Others have a very natural way of turning the situation round so that Adam is put in the spotlight but in a positive way – 'And Adam I'll need you to do the timing for me . . .', thereby circumventing further turmoil. You know your strengths but in the case of constant disruption always proceed with very clear and consistent warnings so that the student has the opportunity to correct his or her behaviour before moving to the next level. Even though they know they are behaving in an unacceptable way, students hate being treated – as they see it – unfairly. If you've warned them of the consequences, then follow through; they have no come back and know it.

If the problem does escalate, and you need to remove a student to get the class settled, proceed with caution. Firstly, make sure you are aware of the school policy – some schools do not allow pupils to be sent out of a room as they often go AWOL and present further, possibly more damaging, havoc around the school. Secondly, if it is common practice to stand errant students outside classrooms, be careful as there may be a whole load of other 'mates' to mess about with out in the corridor. This will create even more problems for you or neighbouring colleagues. Thirdly, it is very common, particularly with a class you're getting to grips with, to forget completely to go out and deal with the student who, in some cases, may be left standing outside for the rest of the lesson.

If possible, it is much better to call on the help of a nearby teacher (who you know has good control) or head of department to take the student off your hands for a short time. Deliver the indvidual swiftly to the classroom or send a runner to request a pick-up. If it's appropriate, pop back and negotiate either the terms for that student returning to your room or the work to be done in the room that he or she has been removed to. The teacher in charge there may have already talked to the individual and have decided whether or not he or she will be returning (depending on the response and the history of the student's behaviour). If the teacher does volunteer to follow up any problems, do take up the offer. Pretending that you're coping only demonstrates a weakness to the pupil whereas seeing you operate as a team, means that there is nowhere to run.

Removing a student for a short spell while you get the rest of the class organized is sometimes all it takes to calm things down. In a school where expectations are high, a student might feel embarrassed and worried that she or he will be seen by a regular member of staff who might take things further or express surprise at the sending out – possibly a bigger punishment if the student respects that teacher. It might be just the time you need to be able to pop out and reason, giving the student the option to come in and make amends so that the matter can be forgotten rather than taken any further. When you do get a moment to talk to the student, focus on the behaviour you want to see when the student returns rather than ranting on about what he or she did wrong. Explain calmly but firmly what it was you found unacceptable if the student demands to know. Avoid being lured into any arguments about what anybody else was or wasn't doing and steer clear of the temptation to get into a blame game. Instead state clearly what you want, allow the student to grumble but then focus the individual on what's going to happen next. The student can make the choice. The conversation might run something along the lines of

> 'I know you weren't the only one, but you were speaking when I had specifically asked you not to. I'm not arguing about it anymore, the rest of the class are working now, I'd like you to come in and get on too and then I'll be happy. I'm not blaming you, I just want you to come in, sit next to Euan and finish the work' (you might need to explain the work here rather than back inside where your pupil will feel self-conscious and your talking might disturb the class) 'and that's the end of it okay? Will you do that? Good!'

If you feel the occasion warrants, you may provide a rider of what will happen if the student chooses to behave inappropriately again but always try to end on a positive steer:

> 'If you do decide you're not going to do as I've asked Nicola, or start yelling over to Holly again then I'm going to ask Mr Rogers to have you in his room for the rest of the lesson okay? But having talked to you, you seem like a sensible person and I'm sure you're going to go in and just get the work done eh . . .'

The other danger with sending out a student is that by being out of your jurisdiction, he or she is liable to cause more havoc.

It's a good idea to glance up and down the corridor before letting anyone out. If the classroom door has a window, be aware that the student may use it to disrupt from outside by appearing at the window and pulling faces to disrupt the rest of the group. To counteract any further nuisance when you are in the process of sending a student out, issue a warning of further consequences; this can be delivered either as the student leaves or actually outside the room depending of the nature of the problem.

With some classes, students might leave without a fuss; others might need you to accompany them out. Tell the student where to stand and quietly explain that if you see his or her face at the door there will be further consequences – be specific. By specifically stating that you do not want to see his or her face at the door, you save yourself the argument of later explaining what they are doing wrong again. Look for patterns of behaviour such as students slamming the door as they leave – they tend to be universal – and pre-empt them. If you are near the door open it for them, then close it behind them.

Rewards

With rules come rewards and sanctions – without them there is no leverage. In some schools supply staff are well supported by class and year group heads. In others you might find support patchy, varying from teacher to teacher or between departments. In some, it will be up to you! It is a good idea to establish beforehand with teachers/colleagues or heads of departments what kind of rewards and sanctions you have at your disposal.

Stickers, stamps and funny faces are all welcome rewards and will keep younger children motivated and keen to work for you in the future. Highlight the potential for stickers at the beginning of the day or lesson, specifying exactly what you're looking for – a table working independently, questions 1 to 5 finished, 100 words written – so that the incentive is there from the beginning. Stickers go down very well with primary classes and can be motivating with students at secondary schools usually for their novelty value – though I generally avoid using them at this level because they are more frequently viewed as being 'babyish'. Even if their novelty works, the stickers can end up in all kinds of places, often worn on the foreheads of students walking down the corridor having left your class in a state of excitement, which doesn't reflect well on you.

With very young children, cuddly toys and games boxes are great motivators – perhaps blue table will be allowed 10 minutes after lunch playing games from the games box (any simple board or card games) as they have done everything as asked. Puppets are a staple of many Key Stage 1 teacher's repertoire and work brilliantly for supply staff – let your imagination run! Games are amazingly powerful with younger secondary students too, who will fly through work in order to have 10 minutes playing at the end of a lesson. I usually take a basic game and adapt it to be subject specific, but that is not crucial.

Class points, team points, merits or credits motivate and reward students and it's worth finding out early on how the reward system operates at the school, how to administer it and the value of a unit. At one school I have worked in, KS3 earn merits for small, manageable tasks well executed such as completing a piece of work or working cooperatively in a team; but at KS4 the awards are geared towards consistently good work sustained over a period of time – to give an award for being particularly good in a lesson would be vastly disproportionate and inappropriate.

Check to see if the school operates separate systems for outstanding work and good behaviour. In this case a note in the planner for parents and tutors, or a positive referral to the regular teacher might be a better option. Students who are constantly in trouble and used to their negative behaviour being reported on will usually be pleased to have a positive comment in their journal, no matter how indifferent they may at first seem. Another way around the issue of remembering a variety of reward schemes is to create your own. However, unless you are with one class for a specific amount of time, this has to be rewarded within one lesson as it can't feed into a greater scheme. On the whole it's better to support the whole-school system.

Most secondary schools these days operate a system of credits or merits that are collected in the school planner and it is a good strategy when first greeting a class to get them to have their planners out on desks (a usual requirement) 'open at the credit page'. This not only focuses the pupils on how they can gain a credit but also means that if they work particularly well (or misbehave) you have their planner to hand to write in any notes to tutors and parents. Try to keep the tone positive and do reward the behaviour that you want when you see it; if most of the class come in quietly, get their equipment out and listen quickly reward the initial few to have done so; as the first students complete a section of work award a credit. This way you alert the class that rewards are available and those who weren't immediately on-task might suddenly feel inspired to get organized or at very least their attempts at disruption will probably fall on deaf ears.

Referral slips

Referral slips are most frequently used in secondary schools, though very large primaries may also use them to track pupils' behaviour. They are used to record both positive and negative behaviours. Find out what the system is and carry around a bunch of slips to fill out for any incidents. It is not uncommon for further action not to be taken without a referral slip.

Report cards

Students on report are usually under pressure to personally ensure that their card or booklet is filled out during the day and will usually be eager to make themselves known to you early on in the lesson. This might take the form of handing you the report and explaining what you need to do or throwing it, dog-eared and folded into the smallest possible size, in your general direction as they enter the room. Make sure you know to whom the cards belong. If you are concerned that you will forget, it might be better to leave the cards on the desk of the student concerned. Where possible, either at the beginning of the lesson or when the group is settled and working, have a quiet word with each of the students about their targets and what you expect of them during the lesson; focus their attention by asking them what they would like you to write on there at the end of the lesson.

Remember that the targets will probably be quite specific and those are the ones you must comment on. Look at remarks from other teachers to get an idea of how the student is working generally and what it is appropriate for you to write. The point of specific targets is that behaviour is modified over a gradual process, eliminating certain unwanted behaviours a few at a time – so if Emma did stay in her chair for the duration of the lesson as was outlined that must be ticked, even if she did conduct all her conversations from that chair across the classroom at an unacceptable level. Technically, if Peter did arrive on time, with all the correct equipment and didn't shout out, as specified, he has achieved his three targets even though he did no work.

It can be seen as being demoralizing to point out all of the things the student didn't do, particularly for the person in charge of trying to develop and coordinate better behaviour patterns so be careful before you scrawl your complaints all over the report card. Check first of all to see whether other teachers have done the same – some schools encourage it, others are very strict about restricting your feedback to the target set – it may be better to refer the problem by memo although it is fine to let the student know this. The bottom line is that if the behaviour of a student is making it impossible either for you to teach, or for students to learn then that student must be dealt with in the same way anybody else would be, report card or no report card.

Detaining students

Detaining students is one of the most powerful sanctions teachers and supply teachers have in changing the behaviour of difficult students. Legally, students are not allowed to be detained for longer than 10 minutes without 24 hours' notice – as some of your more savvy students will be only too keen to point out – but this is not a problem as the most effective detentions are between two and 10 minutes anyway, just enough to cause inconvenience. Long, protracted detentions are pretty much impossible for supply staff to arrange and see through. They are also ineffective and a waste of your time; students adjust their mindset to staying in and often quite enjoy the undivided attention. Although bonding or getting course-work finished might be of use to permanent staff, as supply teachers we need something that will cause an immediate impact and make misbehaving in class a less desirable option. Losing the first part of a break or a lunchtime is a freedom most students prefer not to forfeit.

I never use the word 'detention' with a class – it has too much stigma and anticipation attached to it. At secondary, and even some primary schools, detentions can hold a sort of trophy value – 'Did you get a detention?' classmates will ask in awe; 'Oi! Tell Olly I won't be there, I've got a detention alright!', someone will proudly yell down the corridor. I even worked in a school where detentions were affectionately known as 'DTs'. There's a thrill, and a roguish glamour connected to detentions that I prefer to avoid. Instead I will say, rather euphemistically, and usually only at the end of the lesson –'Amie I'd like a quick word with you before we go please' or 'Blair I need to talk to you quickly'. If the threat of staying in clearly hasn't worked earlier in the lesson, it's best to not spend the lesson banging on about detentions: seemingly empty words just have the effect of making you look weak and vulnerable. A simple appeal at the end, without using the 'D' word, will suffice in quelling the fight or flight mode. Make your request calm, polite and under-dramatic one; any shouting, pointing or ordering will just play into the melodrama and the whole thing can escalate out of hand, and before you know it your classroom will resemble a re-enactment of a scene from *The Crucible* with students whinnying – protesting their innocence, exclaiming how unfair you've been because you haven't also kept in Natalie and Alex as well and generally hamming it up to maximize full attention seeking capability. A simple request is much more difficult to make a big deal out of. If the student asks 'Why?' or (more usually) 'Am I in trouble?' just say 'No, I just want a quick word with you that's all' in a very reasonable manner; when the student asks 'Why?' again, say 'I'll speak to you in a minute okay', and finish ushering the rest of the class out keeping the situation as calm as you can.

That said, they some will try to make a very public issue of it but just stand your ground. Reactions will differ but be aware of the verbal and physical language. If Robert makes a big fuss about how unfair you are and that he isn't staying to 'no detention' but remains in his seat, then he's just trying to save face in front of his peers and will probably calm down after you've gently shooed any remaining spectators out of the room. Reassure him by pointing out that you didn't say detention but that you just want a 'quick chat' with him. Resist the temptation at this point to conduct the talk there and then in the bustle of everyone leaving as he will just nod an agreement with everything you say, followed by 'Can I go now?' in order to get out with the rest of the class, he does need to be detained.

Others will protest and actually look as if they are going to make a break for it. More often than not primary children don't bother with this tactic as they've usually worked out that a) they're with you next and b) they're not that difficult to track in the playground. Wiser secondary students know that schools are big places with lots of hidey-holes and that supply teachers don't usually make the effort to follow things up.

Never try to physically retain students, certainly not by force and it's best not to by blocking their path or the doorway. For a start this can become a sort of challenge or game to get around you, which again puts you in a vulnerable position. Secondly somebody might get hurt in the ensuing barge-fest. If it looks like a student is going to make a bolt for it, just remind the individual that you only want to talk to him or her briefly and if s/he chooses to leave that you will have no option but to report the incident on and Mr Rich will then deal with the matter. If the student does then decide to leave, make sure that you do report the incident on. In this case, refusing to stay when politely asked is much easier for senior staff to follow up rather than students who have refused to stay because a full-scale row has broken out. It is much more difficult to support staff who have completely lost it – shouting, making threats and generally behaving like the students and winding the situation up, especially if, in a moment of frustration, you've acted unreasonably or thrown in a few insults as well. If you neglect to have the incident followed up, then the next time that student appears in your class, he or she, and all friends, will know that you threaten but don't follow up: this reputation will also spread to other classes.

If for any reason you are unable to follow up the incident then the next time the student does turn up to one of your classes, have a brief but positive one-to-one outside the room: remind the student that you weren't impressed with his or her behaviour last time and this time you want a better lesson and that if you're not happy with the conduct, he or she will be removed from the lesson. This way you have followed up the incident yourself and the class will have seen that. If poor behaviour persists, avoid being in the same position again. Either have the student removed before the lesson ends or have another member of staff arrive before the lesson ends to support you if there is a problem, though this is obviously not always possible.

Once the rest of the class have left you can deal with your detainee(s). If it is just one then it should be straightforward as there will be no audience to hinder the process but be aware also that by keeping in only one student you might be making yourself vulnerable by not having a witness. Male teachers keeping in female students, and females retaining male students can in some cases become an issue. If you have any doubts or fears about this either have one of their sensible friends stay behind briefly, get another teacher involved by popping next door and asking if he or she has a moment to spare or wheel the student into the other classroom. Run through what you are unhappy about, what you want to see next time and explain any further action you will be taking should you deem it necessary. With more than one offender, there's an increased likelihood you'll encounter bravado but by refusing to continue while they are not sitting in their places and listening, they will realize that it only delay matters further. Deal first of all with students who are willing to make amends. If a student is now making an effort to finish the work without making a fuss, let him or her work for a short while – depending on how much of the lesson was spent not working – then let the student go, following a quick recap of what you want to see in the future and a reminder that you are allowing him/her to go because you are satisfied that X,Y and Z have been done to your satisfaction – 'Well done Sam, now you've got all that done in just a few minutes, that's how I want you to work next time you're with me, I'm going to let you go now because you've just got on with this work without a fuss'.

The whole point of the exercise is to make a point in order to correct behaviour, not punish. If the point has been made then let the student go – you deserve your break time too. If, on the other hand, you have been very reasonable throughout the lesson in constantly reminding Sam that a certain amount of the work needs to be done, and you know that he was capable of doing it, then let him work the full 10 minutes and then run through the reminders before he leaves. This is also good for those students who think that making a token gesture will be enough to get them off the hook.

Once the more vocal reprobates have seen that just doing the work quietly will ensure a prompt release they will generally take the hint and get on with the work themselves in which case, at a suitably timed interval you can deal with them.

Don't allow students to take control of the agenda by trying to beg, plead and negotiate with you about when they can go and urging you to look at how much they've done. Only talk to them when you are ready and when they are quiet – 'I'm not going to talk to you while you're making a fuss, just do what you've been asked to do and if you've finished sit quietly until I'm ready'. For persistent whiners, draw attention to the fact that the sooner they get started on the work, the sooner they'll be out. Sometimes, if they think they have no chance of completing what they've asked they'll refuse to start. Explain that you want to see at least some of it done. The bottom line is to keep the control. Often bright students, who have spent the time messing about, will quickly finish the work and then demand to go. Keep them waiting a little time after they've finished to make the point that you are the decision-maker. Less able students who might just be genuinely frustrated might need a bit of guidance to begin with, but when they have shown a willingness to have a go you can decide to let them go. With chatty students who have done the work but disrupted the lesson, but managed to complete the task, I make the point by insisting on two minutes' continued silence from them before they leave – they can either start this immediately or when they've finished moaning – they soon get the message.

Some students will claim that they can't stay in with you because they have another detention. Sometimes this is true and sometimes it isn't. Bearing in mind that it is going to be difficult for you to catch these students again, it's best to still detain them long enough to state your terms and conditions and then let them go – if they are late or deemed absent for their other detention, the chances are they'll pay another penalty there. If you do see the teacher in question you can double-check that the students were actually supposed to be in a detention and pass on your apologies with an explanation – most staff will be supportive.

Make a point to always build bridges before a student leaves. If a student stayed behind and did as asked, then this shows a respect for you and that should be acknowledged. Primary pupils don't usually sulk and if they do they are easily brought out of it by chatting about something else or doing a little job in the classroom for which you can express thanks.

Secondary students are more likely to have a little (or big!) stomp, swear or mutter but remember, it sometimes has to get worse before it gets better. Don't appease them or condone this behaviour but don't react dramatically to it either. It may feel bad or as if you haven't got your message across but you will be amazed at just how many 'wronged' pupils will smile or signal a subtle 'Alright' when they pass you in the corridor later. Don't engage in chit-chat with the students you are keeping behind until they have served their penance. Undoubtedly bonding is a very useful incidental outcome of detentions but only after you have made your point. Then a friendly chat about something other than the lesson – what they're doing at the weekend, that it's their mum's birthday or about the piece of artwork they're carrying round – is a lovely way to end on a positive note. It is often a student's way of indirectly apologizing and your way of demonstrating that you are human.

Using support

There is nothing that bothered me more as head of department than offering support to supply teachers landed with lively classes but not being taken up on the offer. I understand that staff may have felt that they weren't succeeding if they had to ask me to intervene or take students, or that they didn't wish me to lose either teaching or preparation time, but the long view is that classes that have lessons where they are allowed to let usual standards drop are much more difficult to handle in the long run. Being offered support is a real benefit and while it's best not to be running for help over relatively minor incidents, colleagues genuinely don't mind stepping in where necessary. The school or department may have been working really hard to lift or maintain discipline and working with them is one way you can help.

Remember that you are new to the school and to the students and they will be trying it on just as they would if you were a permanent member of staff. Even experienced teachers new to a school still require assistance to get on top of classes, sometimes from less experienced though more established members of staff – that's the way it works and with teams, a united front is the most effective way forward.

To begin with, judge the standards generally sought within the school. If you have seen teachers expecting and getting good behaviour in pockets of the school then you know it's possible. If a teacher or the head of department turn up before the lesson talking in euphemisms – 'They can be a bit tricky', 'Sam is a bit of a character' – take the hint and find out more: what are they likely to do, what is and isn't acceptable and then establish exactly what procedures are best to follow and what support is available. If the colleague says something along the lines of 'any trouble have 'em out', then do exactly that. 'Trouble' is of course a very arbitrary term which varies from school to school and teacher to teacher, but look at the cues around you. In one school I would have no hesitation of passing on a student who has behaved in a way that might be the norm in another school because I know that school has certain expectations that need to be met. Once he or she is out the whole tenor of the class changes and further problems are rare.

In other places the approach may – by necessity – be a much more low key: different students, different backgrounds, different school ethos, but I would still not hesitate to remove anyone preventing the rest of the group working or anyone who was unacceptably rude to me. In all cases, obviously provide a quiet word and a warning first but then refer the issue on rather than persevering in the mistaken belief that you are putting someone out by calling in the reserves; staff would not volunteer if they weren't willing to help. Often they are just relieved not to have been given your cover and mindful of when they've been in that situation themselves.

Calling for assistance

Schools where behaviour is an issue will often have procedures in place for removing uncooperative pupils. Some will be pretty slick and others, might seem to you more of a theoretical exercise than a practical application. Nevertheless, find out exactly how to use the system and use what support you have nearby. Some schools operate a card system where you are given a card that can be given to a pupil in an emergency who will take it to the office. Staff there will notify senior management who will – assuming they are not dealing with problems elsewhere – come to your aid. In other schools you might be asked to phone front desk to get back up. If you are not near enough to an office or another member of staff who can either call or watch you class and you consider the situation to be out of hand, either send a student or use your mobile phone and call the school directly.

Accept that they may be elsewhere fighting fires and may not be available to get to you immediately if at all; have a back-up plan for either soothing the situation or finding another member of staff.

Unacceptable Behaviour

Under no circumstances should you be expected to teach students who have either physically or verbally abused you. Swearing directed openly at you and physical abuse (by this I mean 'incidental' pushing or touching interpreted as deliberate but claimed to be innocent; if it's an intentional blow take yourself into another classroom) are usually straightforward enough cases and students should be removed from the class-room as soon as is possible. In the first instance, ask the students to stand outside then follow the prescribed procedure for calling in senior staff. If the student refuses to move, alert senior management, discreetly if possible, but carry on the lesson as well as you can. Remember that help may not be immediate and turning the heat up – much as you feel you should – won't help you in the long run. If the student senses the end is nigh then the common thinking is most likely to be that there is nothing to lose. This is one of the occasions where you may, to throw in another cliché, need to lose the battle to win the war.

Judging intention is difficult, particularly with a new class, and you need to employ all those skills of experience and instinct to help you respond. I once had a Year 11 student punch the table in anger and frustration and tell me it was my face. Although I couldn't feel sure, I didn't sense danger or feel threatened – even though the lad had been involved in fights in school – and simply directed him back to work as calmly and light-heartedly as I could from a distance! Actions speak louder than words (particularly in the case of teenage boys!) and the fact that he settled back to his maths work reassured me. Nevertheless I called senior management just to report the case and kept the incident discreet to avoid fuelling gossip and excitement across the class. Although I hadn't openly been strong the message still got through that I dictated the terms of the classroom.

Being respected

Being respected is a strange issue, there can be the feeling that students should automatically show deference to a member of staff and by and large most students do, but this position can never be taken for granted. Bear in mind that when you see students behaving respectfully towards a teacher it will usually be because the teacher has invested time into developing that relationship, riding the ups and downs of the various tests students employ in order to verify credibility before being certified as 'okay'. Sometimes s/he will have built up a very fair but firm reputation over years and older students and siblings have actively promoted the teacher and so they may appear to have gained immediate respect. Very few staff command instant respect and the manner that you deal with situations – being calm, fair and consistent – is the best way to become valued by students. We are all setting a standard for behaviour by the way we behave ourselves and can't expect our charges to act impeccably if we are yelling, being unreasonable or abusive or generally losing it.

Being supported

Supply teachers and cover supervisors often lament that they don't feel they are backed up in cases where they feel that student attitudes towards them have been inappropriate and this can be a very controversial issue. What often muddies the waters is when staff somehow become inextricably caught up in a fracas or let something minor get out of hand. I have been the situation more than once when a member of staff has called for me to intervene in a student's poor behaviour and having listened to the recounts found myself thinking that had I been spoken to in such a manner I might also have reacted as the student has! Keep issues in perspective and watch actions rather than listen to words. Muttering under their breath, rolling eyes or even 'shooting daggers' are all harmless if the student is getting around to doing what has been asked. When a student does what was required (even if it wasn't without delay), quietly express thanks or praise without a fuss. You are not and won't be seen as being weak by the rest of the class: what they will notice is that the character that always causes havoc in the class is not only getting on with work but has been denied the opportunity to publicly humiliate the teacher. If, on the other hand, the student continues to be unreasonable in spite of your fair requests, seeking support should be a relatively uncomplicated affair.

Problems occur most frequently when staff become personally embroiled in rows with students. If in the heat of the moment a member of staff has been verbally abusive or threatening or ridiculed a student, it can be seen as provocation. The rule of thumb is to stay calm, make reasonable requests and be prepared to explain them. Avoid getting into blame games and concentrate on the behaviour and activity that you would like to see.

Checklist

- Ooze confidence – it's good for both you and your students.
- Learn to use your voice effectively to gain and maintain control.
- Sending pupils out should be a last resort but can help sometimes in getting a class settled.
- Use rewards to encourage good behaviour.
- Fill out referral slips for students who have misbehaved during lessons; not doing so only allows them to repeat the behaviour elsewhere.
- Keep students on report conscious of what is needed to do to get the boxes ticked.
- Keep students back during break or lunch period to make your point – make the experience short and positive.

- Always make sure that any students you do keep in have five minutes towards the end of break time to get a drink and go to the toilet.
- Use support offered by regular staff.
- Use the on-call system if necessary
- Act immediately if you feel you have been physically or personally verbally abused.
- Remember respect takes time to build.
- Avoid getting into heated debates with students. If you feel things are getting out of hand, remove the student or refuse to continue without a third party.
- Ultimately, if you feel that you are not being supported talk to your agency.

11
TEACHING PRACTICAL SUBJECTS

Check with your agency or union if you are uncomfortable delivering practical sessions and be clear with schools and agencies of what you are willing to undertake. For some subjects you may not be legally covered to take a lesson. This could leave you uninsured and unprotected should an accident occur in a lesson you have been in charge of. Sometimes a school may ask you to step in as an extra body while a qualified teacher leads the session.

Depending on your teaching background, your response to covering practical subjects may range from absolute joy to unmitigated horror! Personally I'm quite partial to covering practical lessons for a number of reasons. Firstly students usually see them as a treat. They are quite motivated, not necessarily to *do* the work, but to retain the privilege of 'being free' to do something practical. Secondly, practical subjects usually have very clear stages with tangible ends that need to be met progressively. This helps develop a sense of control. For instance in drama, everybody has to remove shoes, place them next to the wall, then sit in a circle before the lesson begins and in art the tables and floor must be clear before the equipment is given out. Finally, these are often lessons where students are cultivating something that means a great deal to them. They have a personal motivation to do well and because they are capable of working and talking, they feel relaxed about the work. These are often the lessons when you can get to know a little more about the personalities in your charge; their lives, their experiences of school and what makes them tick. Conversely, they are also often the lessons where the students get to see you in a different light, as you sit helping someone to unpick a section of their textiles that has 'gone wrong', or chat as you admire an ongoing piece of artwork and find out how it came about – suddenly you're an 'alright teacher', a compliment which will pay dividends.

Unfortunately there are flipsides to teaching practical subjects. If you are not completely comfortable and therefore not convincing there is no shortage of potential mishaps and madness just lying in wait! To begin with there isn't that reassuring sense of control that can be artificially contrived when everyone is sitting down in their place and will not be required to move until the lesson is finished. Practical subjects provide numerous excuses to move across the classroom: a student splodging everyone en-route with a daub of the green paint he or she just happens to be carrying or disturbing everyone by lunging in between composing pairs and bashing random notes on their keyboard, or turning off someone's computer (and losing the unsaved work) 'just for a laugh'.

Then there are the resources – a dual-pronged hazard. There is no limit to the mischief that can be caused by glue, scissors or sewing needles; even a simple written exercise in a practical classroom can be disrupted by gas and water taps which are just waiting to be turned on and misused.

If you have been asked to oversee practical activities (rather than the safer option of worksheets that could keep any group occupied for the rest of their school life), there's the possible added difficulty of locating the correct resources. In some cases the teacher will have kept the task minimal and all the materials and equipment required will be neatly stacked (often labelled and numbered) in one of those bright yellow poly-corrugated collapsible boxes.

With classes where everyone has embarked on a different project, you may find yourself trying to manage a series of requests for items of which you have no idea of the whereabouts. At this point there will no doubt be a volley of cries volunteering help, advice and knowledge, but unless the class seem very sensible it is probably best to at least check with a neighbouring member of staff before allowing the keys to the stockroom to become available to all and sundry. You can guarantee that there will be opportunists at every level who have been dying to get their hands on the materials box, try out that expensive gouache set aside exclusively for the sixth form, or create an impromptu cupboard orchestra with the glockenspiel, triangles, maracas and one of the ridged wooden fish that are always reserved for someone sensible and are therefore highly alluring.

The best way of ensuring a reasonable practical lesson is to keep it structured: nothing is going to happen until you have established exactly what will be going on in the lesson and even that won't happen until you have everybody's undivided attention. Go through the instructions clarifying anything you or the students are unsure about, allocating tasks and responsibilities, explaining what to do if students either finish or get stuck and warning of consequences for anyone not doing what they should be doing (usually packing up and going to another teacher). When everyone is clear, then you can supervise the proceedings but not before describing exactly what the classroom will look like before the class leave; this will help keep minds focused when it comes to disposing of rubbish – someone who is aware that they personally will be picking up every last thread of snipped cotton or sliver of trimmings from *Hello!* magazine is more likely to stop them landing on the floor in the first place.

It's very useful to have planned feedback sessions throughout the lesson where individuals or groups report back on their development so far and their next step or, if the group is generally involved and working quietly, arrange for a quick gathering at the end where progress can be shared: this gives the group a motivation to concentrate on work as well as socializing. Finally, allow enough time for clearing up, and be precise and insistent that everything goes back where requested and that the room is left intact. It is better to have a little time left over to discuss work, play a game or even just chat than leaving the space untidy and equipment still scattered.

PE

Only qualified teachers of PE are allowed to teach it at secondary level. Unless you are supply teaching in a primary school or a qualified PE teacher you should not be asked to cover a practical session of PE.

Drama

At primary you may well be asked to cover drama. For drama at secondary school, staff are usually asked to provide non-practical work unless specialists are covering. Worksheets or written projects are unusual at KS3 so your biggest problem might be pupils resentful that they aren't going to get to play games or work on a performance they've been developing.

If you are happy to take drama sessions, say so, and have a supply of games and activities on hand. Good groups will organize their own drama games – ones they have learned during the course – but if they seem unsure or the game is veering in the wrong direction, step in with your own. Stick with the usual drama rules – taking shoes off, sitting in a circle to begin – and be firm with poor behaviour. This is one subject where noise and inappropriate activity levels can soar if left unchecked and it can be very difficult to regain control.

Other subjects

Most other practical subjects can easily be turned into non-practical sessions. For example, there are usually textbooks or worksheets to supplement practical science and music; and at secondary, you should not be asked to conduct anything other than theory. Music departments with keyboards or computers and headphones may well set practical composing sessions, but this can be treated as an ICT lesson – basically making sure everyone treats the equipment respectfully. Throughout the lesson, use feedback sessions to share work done so far; this gives students the chance to check they are on the right lines and you an opportunity to monitor their progress. In subject areas such as science and design technology where students are surrounded by equipment, keep an eye out for people fiddling with equipment they shouldn't be touching. Generally in science, students are used to theory lessons. Technology teachers are usually extremely organized and have drilled pupils so well in paperwork procedures that you may feel like a spare part.

Primary practicals

As a primary specialist, you may be asked to cover any number of practical subjects but teachers tend to leave lessons that are simple to cover and often involve ongoing work that pupils are already engrossed in. At least, if things do go awry, you have the power to move on to the next subject a little earlier or return to the numeracy work the class weren't able to complete fully because of an assembly.

Checklist

- Check with your union if you are unclear or uncomfortable about which subjects you may be asked to cover.
- Specify with the school or agency if you are willing to cover practical subjects and if so, which ones.
- Keep order by imposing a clear structure and insist that criteria are met.

In the right hands, computers can be the supply teacher's best friend. Even the smallest of primary schools now have at least one room of PCs. At secondary, it is common for every department to have, if not their own computer suite, access to one shared within a faculty. Many teachers, wishing to make lives easier for both themselves and you will go to great lengths to book a computer room, particularly if their group is a difficult one. They know that working on the computer is – in most cases – an activity still regarded by many students as 'not proper work', though there are classes that have had so much exposure to the ICT suite that they would welcome something different – like working from a book!

To log onto a network, you will typically need a username and password. In smaller schools the class teacher may simply pass on his or her details, but in larger schools log on details will have been set up for supply staff. It is a good idea to find out this information as early as is conveniently possible when starting at a school. This is particularly important if you spot IT on your timetable for the day! It is perfectly possible to conduct an IT lesson without actually logging on yourself but having access to the system often allows you the opportunity to have a little more control. In some cases you will be able to switch access to the internet on and off and, for those familiar with the program, some systems permit the monitoring of different students from the teacher's computer.

In my experience, ICT lessons planned for cover teachers are usually sound. Practitioners of the subject are usually thorough and logical in their guidance and often use programs or sites that explain step-by-step what needs to be done – but maybe I've just been lucky! Problems can occur when other teachers have arranged for their groups to 'finish coursework' or 'carry on research'. It is a good idea to start by establishing your own expectations of what you want to see by the end of the lesson – that may be a number of words that will have been typed up or that individuals will be asked to present their findings or read aloud a paragraph of their work.

It is also as well to establish at this point which programs are, and are not, acceptable during the lesson, especially if you have no way of turning off the internet. My general rule of thumb is to offer 'free' time for the last 10 or 15 minutes of the lesson provided I am happy with the amount of work done and conduct of the group or individual.

Where possible I block the internet or have it blocked by another teacher or IT technician (beware that in some cases this cannot be done if a student has already logged on so find out before anyone gets started) to save the inevitable temptation. Where this is not possible, perhaps because the work set requires internet access, I also promise 'free' time at the end. In all cases I make clear that students who are on the web when they shouldn't be or are on an inappropriate site will simply log off and I will set some alternative work. This usually does the trick.

There are some lessons, where so little detail has been left or where students seem to finish what they have been asked to do, that there is very little you can do other than allow free time on the internet. In these cases it is as well to have a few sites up your sleeve ready and waiting. Divide the time up to go on each of the sites then allow 'free time' for those who have stuck to your guidelines.

See page 143 for suggestions of reliable sites and no doubt you will find some of your own. You can depend on some sites, such as the BBC, but even that is not foolproof. There is a lovely magnetic poetry-type activity on the BBC where users can choose to create poems from themed words on subjects such as *Gothic, Space Travel, Wildlife, Love* – the first three are great but some of the boys in my Year 8 class were thrown into a frenzy when they saw the word 'sex'! When in doubt, stick to children's sites but always do your research beforehand. Another advantage of having tried sites yourself is that you will know which activities are worth pursuing. You will also be able to set up specific challenges to help avoid mindless and fruitless explorations of a site. I frequently use maths sites, of which there are plenty and which provide fun games and puzzles, but there are so many that students often just flick briefly through a game, then move on to try another. Select a couple of games and set a target for either individuals or pairs with a reward – a merit, smiley, sweet (see pages 67 and 115 for more on rewards). For example on coolmath.com there is a game called

RUSH where the player has to get a green car out of a garage by juggling various other vehicles backwards and forwards; I either offer a reward to the pair who score the highest level or for anyone who gets to a certain level, depending on the year group. Another game on the mymaths website is called How Big Is Your Brain, where players follow then copy a pattern of coloured lights. The target is to gain status of 'Maths Mogul' which again can be an individual challenge or a competitive game where two or more players take it in turns to copy losing lives for every mistake made. If you have an interactive whiteboard this game lends itself well to a whole-class challenge where pairs can practise and then come up to the board to compete for real.

Should you ever be in a computer suite without work and an armoury of useful sites, you can always ask students to research a topic or sites that help them learn and then ask them to report back their findings and rate the sites in terms of suitability for different age groups. Have them write a 200 word report comparing three different sites. Keep an eye on sites visited. Although LEA filter systems are generally overprotective, some website designers are very good at bypassing filters and some students are very knowledgeable when it comes to sneaking past filters too.

Behaviour/Procedures

For all of their advantages, computer rooms also have a habit of being notoriously difficult to teach in. Excited at the prospect of being on a computer and determined to get the best seat, students often stream in, energized and frantic, pushing, shoving and trying to bag a seat for their best friend. In the frenzy, buttons and keyboards are jabbed at inconsiderately, mice swapped over and all kinds of damage can be wreaked in the first five minutes.

The layout of IT suites also often make it difficult to gain and maintain undivided attention: students usually face away from you, often tucked into corners and you have to view the class over ranks of computers and you are obviously competing against whatever is going on onscreen. With this in mind it is always best where possible firstly to talk to the class away from the computer room so that you can establish your expectations of behaviour, outline rewards and sanctions and perhaps explain work. So if you are taking a primary group, start in the classroom if one is available. If you have to meet the group in the ICT room, try to set some guidelines before even letting the class in – perhaps that you want the group to just find a seat and not log on, or that they may log on but then must switch off screens and be ready to listen to you. Anybody not following the agreed guidelines should immediately log off and you will discuss whether or not they can log on again. However well organized you are, there will always be a rise in noise when the class first settle. It is usually only chatter while they wait for the computers to warm up and log on; afterwards the class will calm down as they become absorbed in their own work. Just cast an eye round to make sure the noise is just chatter and accept that it will recede as they settle.

It can be awkward to get attention once the class is going. This is for the usual reasons but also because what's going on on-screen is bound to be of more interest than whatever you're about to say, even if it is the answer to the question they've all been individually asking! Get the group into a habit of turning off their screen and turning to face you, hands on lap, off keyboards. There will be the sneaky one or two that think it's okay to press another couple of buttons or even carrying on regardless. Again, getting them to log off and come and sit closer to you, away from the computer, will make your point clear.

Computers going wrong

The only other thing to remember when teaching IT is that computers are not infallible and seem to have a sixth sense which is why you can bank on them to breakdown either partially or wholly when you have the most difficult class you've come across all day. With just a few computers presenting problems it's always possible to double students if they are of a mind to work together. Where this is not possible or convenient

– perhaps the internet is 'temporarily' unavailable (and has been for the past three hours) – it might be better to cut your losses and pull out one of your pre-prepared one-offs (if the teacher hasn't already set a back-up plan). Just be prepared – computer lessons can be like mother's milk on a good day but must never be trusted to deliver the goods – only you can do that.

Lessons moved to computer rooms

Benevolent staff often arrange for cover lessons to be relocated to ICT suites in order to lessen the burden of the supply teacher, who instead of having to teach a lesson will be able to organize and support. I have often been appreciative of this gesture, particularly with challenging classes or unfamiliar subject areas. If you arrive at your English class to find that the teacher has asked that the group goes to Z20 to complete coursework or the RE department or that you take 9E to IT room 4 to interact with a series of interactive websites, your heart should jump for joy. But be wary, such a move still needs thoughtful organization.

To begin with, get the class into their usual room to register them and explain what will be happening today. You have more chance of getting their undivided attention here. It's much easier to address a group settled in a familiar room with few distractions than having to compete with concerns about who's sitting where and keys to press on keyboards. Besides, it's more difficult to gain full attention when a class is sitting behind banks of monitor. With younger pupils you might even use their initial behaviour to decide whether they are actually going to get computer time or five minutes free time at the end of the lesson. Beginning the lesson in the usual room grants you that slight leverage; the promise of time on the computers is generally seen as a treat and as such classes are much more likely to comply with your expectations and guidelines for behaviour.

Register the group. While you are doing this, it might be prudent to have a trustworthy type to go to the computer room and check that the room is a) open (so you don't arrive with

30 excited Year 7s only to find it locked without a key to hand), and b) not occupied. There are certain times of year in secondary schools – usually after the departure of Year 11 – when the ICT timetable becomes a bit of a free-for-all and there is no set procedure for bookings, or the science department have sequestered all computers for Science Coursework Week. Your runner can always be dispatched to find another ICT room should there be an issue with room availability. In the meantime, having registered the group, you can run through the work that needs to be done, your expectations of how much will have been completed, your feedback plan and any incentives or sanctions on offer. This is a good time to anticipate any potential problems while you have the attention of the whole class. There may be some queries you can effectively deal with, such as the fact that Yasmin hasn't been here and doesn't 'have a clue what to do' – pair Yasmin with someone who has agreed to explain it all to her. This should save you the job or having to deal with such issues when you actually arrive at the ICT room when, no doubt, you will be busying yourself overseeing the scrum and sorting out the computers.

You should also remind the group of types of behaviour you would like to see and sanctions for anybody not towing the – very reasonable – line. If resources (exercise books or notes) need to be ferried to the room, arrange for their transit, either letting Brian and Angela take them as usual or giving them out there and then. Finally, establish exactly how you intend the group to make their way there, bearing in mind that changes in room often generate over-enthusiasm and that the rest of the school will, by now be working and whether the group can go in and get started or if they need to line up and wait for you. Sending the groups in small groups at a time, sensible first means that the arrival – and therefore the scrum to get in – will be staggered and possibly slightly calmer. Alternatively it might be is wiser to actually escort the group yourself if you have any doubts about behaviour; that way you can ensure that nobody takes a long cut or repairs to the loos for a crafty drag en route. Make sure that you know how to get to the room – it's too easy to let small groups go and then realize you can't remember the way.

If necessary, leave time at the end of the lesson to have resources returned to the original room or pack up early enough to get the whole class back to base. Make sure, as always, that chairs are tucked back under desks in every room you have used.

ICT – Games

www.bubblegumclub.com

www.yahooligans.yahoo.com

www.freeonlinegames.com

www.stickcricket.com

www.knoxskorner.com (blue 'dough' figures)

www.coolmath.com

www.mymaths.co.uk

13

WRITING
ACROSS THE
CURRICULUM

Where a straightforward comprehension exercise has been left, challenges are not complicated to set – completing a section or a certain number of questions by a particular time are achieveable targets. With writing, things aren't quite as straightforward, although I find that setting a number of paragraphs with a specified number of sentences per paragraph, usually creates the direction needed. I either specify National Curriculum levels at Key Stages 2 and 3 or, if it's English, GCSE grades. If I'm unfamiliar with the group ability, targets range from 'excellent' to 'good' and 'okay'. These can be jazzed up to suit the students' motivation by using terms that they relate to – computer game 'pro' 'expert' 'rookie' or footballing 'premiership' 'first division' 'down the park', etc. The idea is to get the class to select their own individual targets so that they are specifically accountable throughout the lesson. After all, a paragraph can be any number of sentences – when someone has spent most of the lesson chatting they can still claim to have written a paragraph. The challenges are actually fairly arbitrary but they are usually successful in motivating students to write – they are so focussed on hitting the target that they cease to worry about what to write. Amending and editing are so much easier once there are words on the paper. The most difficult problem, as any teacher knows, is getting something down in the first place. So, depending on age and ability I select challenges such as:

	KS4	KS3	KS2
Top	11–15 sentences	8–12 sentences	5–8 sentences
Middle	8–12 sentences	5–8 sentences	4–5 sentences
Bottom	5–8 sentences	4–5 sentences	3–5 sentences

This is a very rough guide but generally works. Students, suddenly offended by such constraints, always seem to ask if they can write more, which of course you reluctantly agree to! I'm not sure whether it's pride, or peer competitiveness but most students will pick either a target that suits them or one higher. If they select something well below their capability, it is easy to spot and to step in and hike up the target a level or two as they are doing so well. Initially simply praise completion of the number of sentences then, as the work mounts up, discuss the content if necessary.

With either Literacy or English, I sometimes throw in other challenges such as varying sentence beginnings or including x-number of 'excellent' words (you may need to agree with the class beforehand on the definition of an excellent word, taking a few examples from the group and getting them to gauge them as brilliant, good and okay) or punctuation. These features will not only improve the writing but will be easy to check on: *'Richard, read me your sentence-beginnings so far ... great.' 'Nishal, how many excellent words do you have? Read them out.' 'Ellie, how many excellent words do you need to add?'* and so on. These keep maximum focus with minimal effort on your part as you can conduct editing without having to read everybody's work separately.

	Sentence Beginnings	Punctuation
Top	All sentences begin with different words.	Full stops, commas, speech marks and capital letters are correct and some other types of punctuation used (brackets/hyphens/ exclamation marks, etc.)
Middle	Most sentences begin with different words.	Full stops, commas, speech marks and capital letters are correct.
Bottom	Some sentences begin with different words.	Full stops and capital letters are correct.

14
USEFUL TIPS

Confusion can set in quickly when you're flitting around from school to school. Even when you are fairly familiar with the way things run, students begin to look like each other and the subtle differences such as whether diaries are known as 'diaries', 'planners' or 'journals', rewards are 'merits' or 'credits', lessons are 40, 50 or 60 minutes long can become blurred, especially if it's been a frantic morning or a very late night.

School folders

It's a good idea to build up a portfolio of schools – a folder for each – to contain any information you have received from the school (staff handbook, map, staff listings) where you can also store any other related information such as incident or accident reports, copies of claim forms. A handy reference card is another simple but invaluable tool. Admittedly it's no major problem if you do refer to planners rather than journals and your classes won't suddenly revolt, it's just that getting it right means your transition to regular member of staff becomes more seamless in the eyes of the students who otherwise love to pounce on anything slightly different to what they're used to. Getting lesson timings wrong is a bigger issue and is an easy mistake to make when you take into consideration the seemingly erratic time-tables some schools have – two-week schedules; shorter lessons on Wednesdays; celebration assembly every third Thursday – and that's before you've factored in multiples of schools!

Interactive whiteboards

Interactive whiteboards are still objects of wonder at some secondary schools but at primary are almost old hat. Interactive whiteboards really are fabulous teaching tools and if you don't know how to use one, find out. See if you can get a member of staff to spend a little time to run through the applications, and spend a lunchtime getting to grips with it. It will be time well invested. Not only will you be able to tap into the potential, you won't feel embarrassed when the Year 3s have to explain to you which motifs to click on!

If you are pretty IT savvy, you might like to bring in some of your favourite resources on a memory stick. You might also be able to take any away to use elsewhere. Check with the IT coordinator that it is okay for you to do so, before you go spreading any viruses.

15

ACTIVITIES

Useful activities

Every day, supply teaching brings something different and unless you know what kinds of lessons and which age ranges you will be teaching, it is very difficult to have ideas for lessons prepared beforehand. If you are fortunate enough to be teaching your subject at secondary or your age range at primary, you will probably already be familiar with the kind of things you might do should you be left without any lesson plans. However if, like many supply teachers, you end up covering lessons all over the place it is as well to have a rough plan that you can adapt to suit any age or any subject, either by using the framework but altering the content to match the class or altering the pace or both. For these reasons the activities suggested here are accordingly ambiguous and tend to be skills-based rather than subject specific. Some make great starters but would also work as the main section of a lesson with groups working at a slightly slower pace. It is difficult to present a definitive list of one-off lessons for such a broad audience from primary age to secondary, ranging across all subjects. Different personalities suit different approaches too. These are the bare bones of activities – they can be dressed up or down to suit the occasion.

Some activities listed might warrant further research depending on your previous experience and knowledge; others may already be familiar or act a springboard for you to vary and adapt. A number of the ideas listed here are trademarked or copyrighted – this means that you will need to invest in books, or borrow them from the library, to get at the activities but it is well worth the investment in time and/or money.

Don't be afraid to try out new ideas, especially when everything seems to be going wrong. In my experience, necessity is certainly the mother of invention, and many of my activities have been in a moment of divine inspiration, just in time to divert a class from a seemingly inevitable riot!

Finally, a note regarding keywords: keywords are one of the most useful resources to have to hand. In the back of the *National Strategy* for secondary schools folder are lists of subject spelling – these can be used for most of the word games. Look out for textbooks that contain key concept lists too and jot them down to add to your collection. At primary, classroom walls are some-times adorned with the words being used for current topics and teachers can usually give you lists. In the back of *The National Literacy Strategy* folder are high and medium frequency words.

A to Z

This activity is a great starter or plenary. You could extend it into an investigation with the use of resources. It also lends itself to a quiz or competition format, awarding the team with the most plausible answers.

The students jot down the letters of the alphabet (or you prepare a photocopy that they can fill in). Working either alone or in groups of two or three, they think of words related to the given topic beginning with the letters of the alphabet. This means that the exercise can be used very generally – for example 'music' or 'maths' – or more specifically – 'Tudors' or 'Christianity'.

Acrostics

This is a variation of 'A to Z' but allows the letters chosen to appear anywhere within the word.

nu**M**ber
r**A**tio
frac**T**ions
pie c**H**art
perc**E**ntage
diagra**M**
Algebra
pat**T**ern
equat**I**on
cir**C**les
Symmetry

Anagrams

A good starter: use keywords in an anagram form and the class untangles them. Even better, can the class turn keywords or subject concepts into humorous anagrams, attempting to transform the words into other words or phrases?

Bag of words

Have a pre-prepared bag of words. You might choose to colour code the cards so that verbs, adverbs, adjectives and nouns can be easily identified should you wish to eliminate or specify certain types.

As a verbal game, pass the bag around the circle or class and when you say stop the student holding the bag takes a word from the bag and the rest of the class make sentences using that word.

Variations

- If the words are simple, they can be translated into French or if you are a languages teacher you can adapt the bag to a simple languages lesson.
- If you are warned ahead of time or can make the cards during the lesson, the words can be keywords that the student or pairs can define and explain.
- With a combination of types of words, use six randomly chosen ones to begin each sentence in a paragraph, or six words to be used anywhere within a six-sentence paragraph.

Beat the teacher

Not with a big stick, but to the end of the word. Taking it in turns, you and the class add letter by letter to any given starting letter with the aim of completing the word. If either side believes the other has added a letter that couldn't possibly lead to a word in the English language, then they can challenge their opponents. If the side under suspicion can justify their letter by declaring the word they had in mind, if it is indeed a word, that party wins. If it isn't, or isn't spelled correctly, the other side gets the point. With practice, this becomes a game of strategy as it is possible to force the other side to spell out a certain word. It is a good idea to agree from the outset not to use slang, abbreviations or plurals.

Bingo

Similar to Beat the teacher, but start by either getting students to draw a 4 x 6 table, or 4 rows of 6 circles or handing out a pre-prepared sheet of 24 boxes. Then ask the students to number them randomly from 1–24 to create an individual bingo card.

- Read out questions which should then be answered in the appropriate box, depending on the question number. Remember to read the questions in a random order.
- When a student has a full line, check the answers and award a team point or merit. If one or more of the questions are incorrect, you do not have to tell the student which ones are, just continue the game. The game can continue until you have one winner or more.

Book evaluation: exercise books

Talk to the class about the expectations of presentation in the school or in the class. Talk about standard procedures and discuss why they are what they are. Students often don't see the point of dates, titles, learning objectives, page numbers and reference to any exercises undertaken – encourage them to reflect on why they might be useful to teachers and to themselves. Are there rules about ink colour or the use of pencils? Are there ways of keeping a book looking tidy even if your handwriting is untidy? How do they lay out their work?

The class draws up a set of criteria from which to judge the presentation of a book. It will probably include things such as:

Date
Title
Reference to books being used and page numbers
Blue/black pen
Spacing
Writing on every page
Writing that runs from margin to margin
Handwriting

Define poor to excellent for each category and decide on a score structure, perhaps a five-star award system.

Depending on how cooperative the group is, agree whether individuals will assess their own books, swap with a friend or use a completely random redistribution arrangement. It is good for students to reflect on their own work and some classes and individuals would feel too vulnerable to allow someone else to gauge their success. On the other hand, it can be one of the best learning experiences or wake up calls to see other people's work and realize firstly that you could be doing better and secondly just how to do that.

Finally, the students consider their strengths and weaknesses and record them in a short series of bullet points. If the activity is going well and you have time, they feedback to the class what targets they have assigned themselves.

Book evaluation: textbooks

Most classes have some kind of textbook knocking around. If you're lucky, there may be a selection enabling you to turn any lesson into an investigation, getting groups to compare a number of different books or having groups report back on a book which the class can then discuss.

As confident and experienced readers, it is sometimes difficult to comprehend the fact that some students find it incredibly difficult to navigate their way around a textbook, but when examined in close detail, from the point of view of the less experienced reader, it is easy to understand just how complicated and over busy some textbooks actually are.

Begin by discussing how readers navigate their way around a non-fiction book. Get the group to brainstorm ideas – contents page, chapters, headings and sub-headings, page numbers, boxed areas, index. Ask them if they remember coming across any that were clear and easy to follow or particularly difficult.

If you are able to do so 'on-the-hoof' ask the group to locate certain sections without giving page numbers – the chapter on weddings/ exercise 16c, question 4/the map of Europe/how to calculate speed, distance and time/the diagram of the knee joint. Make sure that the fastest people do not shout out the page numbers.

Ask the group to reflect on what made the process of pinpointing the sections specified easy or difficult. Record their thoughts and throw in a few more points to consider: font, font size, colours, position of page numbers, headings, etc.

Do the books you are looking at have a distinct layout? – perhaps extra facts are always in a pink box; questions are always at the bottom of the right-hand page; headings and sub-headings have different colours or fonts or sizes which distinguish their importance. Has the book been designed to help the reader find their way through or just to look exciting?

With the class draw up an agreed formula that could be used in evaluating the clarity of a textbook in both navigating through the book and accessing information – is the text easy to read, easy to follow?

In groups or pairs evaluate a book or selection of books against the criteria, recording scores and comments.

Conduct a feedback session where groups compare their findings – either reporting back group by group or book by book.

As a spin off, classes could design or redesign the page layout of any given book; design the idea layout or write to publishers sharing their findings.

Brain gym®

Brain Gym® has a number of activities that get students engaged and thinking. Many will stimulate your kinesthetic learners, the ones who struggle to sit still for any period of time. They suit all ages and abilities – check it out on the web.

Constructing sentences

Write a sentence that contains:

3 nouns
2 connectives
2 verbs
3 adjectives
2 adverbs

Write a sentence with 17 words, describing an empty beach.

There are endless variations to this activity and not all can be achieved! Model a willingness to have a go and an acceptance that there is no right answer by joining in yourself.

Cognitive diagrams

Teach your class how to draw diagrams to generate, visualize, structure and classify ideas. For problem-solving, decision-making, recording great quantities of information learned and organizing thoughts, Tony Buzan is your man! His book *Mind Maps for Kids* has loads of activities, covering all areas of the curriculum. Perfect for one-offs, starters or for complementing work set.

Countdown

Using the format of the television programme but with a little more thinking time, create word and numerical problems to be solved individually or in pairs.

Words – given a group of nine letters including a minimum of three vowels and a minimum of four consonants, create as many words as possible in three minutes.

Numbers – using four numbers between 1 and 10, plus two from the following: 25, 50, 75 and 100, attempt to make any given three-digit number. Demonstrate by working through a problem with the help of the class. Award points for clever strategies as well as the correct answer.

Drawing

One of my favourite starters is one I was left to do in one of the primary schools I supply in. It is to draw as many things that contain a certain shape (drawn or projected on the board) as possible. It certainly kept the class engaged and coming up with very imaginative ideas. The shape could be a circle, a cross or something more obscure. Projecting it onto a whiteboard means that pupils can take it in turn to come up and draw their best idea onto the whiteboard.

- A 10-minute doodle is a quiet, absorbing activity, nice for settling down a class after lunch. You might need to provide an example to get start unconfident pupils so if you're not comfortable ad-libbing on the board, have 'one that you prepared earlier'!

- Copying a picture upside-down is a great activity for focusing the mind and is often done best by students who will claim they are 'no good at art'. Having to observe the picture upside down forces our brains to translate the image in a different way. This is also a useful activity to give to early finishers – a photograph or picture and piece of paper and pencil.
- Draw an object – the more traditional observational drawing. If you can draw, teach the class how to sketch the lines, work out proportions and look for and replicate shade and light.
- Cartoons are always a favourite. I once picked up a class who had been drawing cartoons with a supply teacher on the previous day and couldn't wait to complete their work and get back to their cartoons. If you know how to teach the drawing of scenes or characters do so; if not, teach how to organize a storyline or outline what you'd like the cartoon to show (something related to the learning, a memory or something completely random) and let the students develop their ideas regardless of their drawing skills.
- Draw what you've learned today. Stress that no formal drawing skills are required – just a personal interpretation of what students have remembered from their work during the lesson or the day, the project or the term.

Hangman

A perennial favourite and ideal for small gaps of time as the games are short and the game doesn't usually need explaining. Words can be restricted to subject-specific. The main problem thrown up by hangman, as with any class game, is the din created if students have not been reminded of the rules of engagement – i.e. not shouting out.

Hot seat

There are many variations to hot-seating – mix and match to suit.

- Person to be hot-seated can be the teacher or student, in role or as themselves. Topics can be factual, factual and imaginative or purely creative. For example students may question the teacher in order to work out the events of a story, incident or an event of historical, social or scientific significance. Question Lady Macbeth about the death of her husband, or Louis Pasteur about his claim to fame. Students might question each other about a project they've been working on or their opinions about something related to that project – for instance, their role in climate change, what they know about Shakespeare or medieval music. The hot-seated character may be someone from history or a book the class are studying or the character may be completely improvised, someone who may be thrashing out his or her identity and background as the questions are fired.

Jeopardy

Give the answers, the students have to devise the question. If you have access to whiteboards, get the students to write their questions on them so that everybody gets a go at answering, even though not all need be read out.

Keywords and concepts

Write six (numbered) categories on the board; a student throws a dice then has to say as many words and ideas related to the particular category in a given number of seconds. Keep the time short (15–20 seconds) and work rapidly round the class.

Lateral thinking

You know the kind of activity – a situation is explained and the audience has to solve the mystery:

- Bob and Ethel are lying dead on the ground, surrounded by glass and water: how were they killed?
- A surgeon goes in to theatre to attend to a young boy who has been brought in after he was involved with his father in a terrible road accident. The father has been killed. On seeing the boy, the surgeon exclaims with horror, 'But that's my son!' Explain the relationship between surgeon and boy.

There are so many sites on the internet, loaded with such puzzles that it's difficult to choose the best. Simply type in 'lateral thinking' and fill up with conundrums to keep a class occupied. Students have a tendency to give up if they cannot automatically work out the answer so think of ways of encouraging them to view the problem from different perspectives. Developing a system to reward all lines of enquiry will also keep discussion open. Let the group work in teams to foster discussion and combat the fatigue that sometimes dogs pupils working alone.

Learning styles

Discussing and reflecting on learning styles can be a real break-through in pupils' approaches to school and is a great one-off lesson to get everybody thinking. Awareness of visual, auditory and kinesthetic learning styles has been around in teaching for some time now but doesn't always reach the classroom in an explicit format, though many teachers do integrate a variety of activities to suit different learners into their teaching. Howard Gardner's *Multiple Intelligences* also strongly influences teaching styles. An understanding of visual, verbal, logical, kinesthetic, musical, interpersonal and intrapersonal learning preferences makes for an interesting lesson, particularly for older students who have a little more control over their learning in preparation for exams. There is a wealth of information and host of self-test quizzes on the web that can be adapted to suit your age range.

Memory games

Use the standard format of repeating what everyone else has said so far, then adding your own idea. Starting lines could be 'What I've learned today', 'What I'd like to learn today', 'I'm going on a picnic and I'm taking ...' . The leader can be topic-focused or aiming to inspire creativity. I've seen the picnic theme used as a problem-solver rather than memorizing what everyone has said previously. The students say what they are intending to take; then the teacher tells them whether or not they are allowed to depending on whether they've picked up on the rule created – without their knowledge – at the beginning. You model the rule, which might be using your initials (Delicious Ham) or two consecutive letters of the alphabet; the students have to try to work it out and fit in. Working your way through the alphabet and memorizing is another version – 'Tonight I'm going to eat an apple, balti, coconut, digestive biscuit, eggs and fried bacon'.

Millionaire

There are a host of quiz books available (particularly at Christmas) that can be used for one-off quizzes. It's worth picking up a couple and having them to hand. Check that the questions are suitable for the age range you are most likely to be teaching beforehand rather than have the activity fall flat on its face when you're in the thick of it. Websites such as the *BBC's NewsRound* has regular quizzes but they tend to be short, so either collect the questions over time or use as fillers. A colleague of mine uses a *Who Wants to be a Millionaire?* quiz and loves playing the Chris Tarrant part with full drama which always goes down well. DVD and TV quizzes can also be utilized if you can rely on the use of a computer, interactive whiteboard or DVD.

Moral dilemmas

Dilemmas are always good for a one-off lesson, particularly if there are few or no resources available. Games in the style of the balloon game (you have to decide which of the famous or useful characters – wise old man, pregnant woman, doctor, engineer, etc. – should be evicted from the balloon, aeroplane or life raft in order for the others to survive.

- Use also personal dilemmas – a starving mother stealing to feed her children; falling in love with your best friend's boy/girl friend; saving one of your two children from certain death.
- Ideally get the group into a circle; if not organize a procedure for everyone to report back and be heard. Run through rules for listening and remind the group that put-downs – comments, sniggers, significant eye contact or gestures at others – will not be tolerated.
- Moral dilemmas are surprisingly difficult to find on the internet so keep your eyes peeled for books and resources from personal, social and health education materials. The following can be used or adapted. Ask students to think of three different responses and follow them through to their possible conclusion:

Your best friend Jake tells you that his dad sometimes hits him – he shows you the bruises. You promise not to tell but see that Jake is becoming quieter and depressed. What do you do?

You find a wallet containing £50 and some credit cards. You would like to buy your mum a lovely present for Mother's Day but are a little short on cash. What do you do?

A friend confides in you that they have committed a crime (in school or out of school) and that he or she is afraid of what will happen if caught. You promise not to tell anyone, but now an innocent person is about to be disciplined and or prosecuted. What do you do?

A very close friend with terminal illness asks you to assist them in suicide. To do so would be against the law but you see that your friend is in a great deal of pain and there is nothing more the doctors can do. What would you do?

163

You are the headteacher of a school that is short on funding but desperately needs more resources. A company with a highly unethical background offers to provide some high-quality resources for maths and English for free, but the resources would have to have the company's logo prominently featured as a source of advertising. You are concerned that doing so would influence your students and you are worried that the school will be seen to be supporting the unethical practices of the company. What would you do?

You are the head teacher of a school. A soft drinks company offer to sponsor the building of a new sports development but only if you agree to not sell any other products in your vending machine and to promote the product in order to sell a minimum number of drinks per month. You are concerned that promoting a sugary drink is not the health message you've been trying to give your students. You do not have the money to build the sports facilities yourself; if you do not accept the sponsorship your students will have to put up with the old resources. What would you do?

Town X is a very pretty coastal town but the residents are poor as there is no local industry to support the population. The town could be developed as a tourist attraction as a place of outstanding natural beauty, which would boost the local economy. However, bringing in tourists would have a largely negative impact on the local environment and ecology with the increase of transport, building of new roads and hotels and general wear and tear of the location. What would you do?

My favourite pastime

Using their own initials, students take it in turns to declare their favourite pastime, being as creative and original as they can be. 'My favourite pastime is Digging Holes', 'My favourite pastime is Designing Expensive Hats' – keep going until you run out of ideas. As a variation, students could introduce the two people sitting on either side of them: 'This is Tony Rogers and his favourite pastime is Tagging Rhinos; this is Claire Coakes and her favourite pastime is Canning Cucumbers'.

Predictive hangman

Loosely based on Hangman, in this activity the steps that lead to the tightening of the noose are not incorrect answers but poor guesses. To this end, the letters have to be guessed in order, so the word is 'spelled' out with underscore lines as in Hangman but the first letter of the word is given. If the guess made is an intelligent guess i.e. the letter could work next to those revealed so far, the player or team either don't lose a life at all or lose only half a life. Keep a record on the board of incorrect guesses and intelligent guesses. The easiest way to judge guesses is to ask the student to explain their thinking. For example, if the next guess for: w h _ _ _ is either 'e' or 'i' both could be plausible so are intelligent guesses, whereas 'k' or 't' are not, so a life is lost. It's probably best for you to adjudicate these games, if not lead them – as teacher you can make fair rulings to suit the ability of your group.

Self-evaluation

As the class to reflect on their performance during the lesson, what have they learned, what have they achieved and how well have they worked? What do they need to do next time to improve? How could they get more out of the lesson? Which parts did they find difficult or easy? Feedback can be oral or written on paper to be handed in or exercise books.

Self-generated quiz

Based on a current topic, or topics studied so far this year, the class each writes a question and answer which can then be handed in and used for a class quiz. If the class is big enough one question each should be enough to last the lesson – by the time you've explained the game, handed out and collected in papers, read and repeated the questions and read out the answers. As a safeguard however you may like to ask each member to actually write three questions and answers just in case there are a number of repeated questions.

If the class or year group generally attend the same lessons, you might extend the topics covered to include any subject on the curriculum, either currently or at any time since they started school. Give some examples. Or, you might ask for one subject question and one general question based on perhaps music or television or sport.

If sport and music are included in the quiz, it is probably best to conduct the quiz as a team affair, mixing boys and girls. If you do choose to use a group format, the group writes the questions together.

The main problem with quizzes is they can engineer a sense of excitement with noise levels to match, so it is as well at the beginning to warn that you only intend to treat the class with a quiz if they are prepared to keep the noise level down. With groups that seem to have potential bouts of boisterousness, get the groups to write their answers rather than conducting a 'call out' or 'hands-up' quiz. If the marking session proves slow because you are battling to get the answers heard amidst cries and yelps of joy, award extra points for quiet groups.

Spelling investigation

- Take any text or texts and select words containing a given letter – for example *c*. The group trawls the passage(s) to find words containing that letter – received; accidentally; active; choir; church; casually; cycled and so on.
- The group then share their findings which should be collated on the board so that the whole group can benefit from the results of others.
- Read, or get the group to read aloud their answers. Read a second or third time, this time listening for how the letter chosen is pronounced. For the case of *c*, there should be hard *c*s (*k* sound – catalogue); soft *c*s (*s* sound – perceive); *CH* (church)

sounds and, possibly, *KW* sounds (*ch*oir). In some cases there may be a combination of sounds (a*cc*ident). Without actually pointing out the relationship between sound and spelling, get the class to group the words into sound categories. Top sets should be able to do this alone but some pupils may require a little help in which case you could specify the categories for them.

- Once sorted, the groups suggest a spelling rule:
  soft *C*s are usually followed by ...
  hard *C*s are usually followed by ... etc.
- Once the rules have been proposed, test their validity by thinking up other words containing *C* to check whether they work in all cases in most cases or only in some cases.
- Write up the rules.
- Ask the students how they could use what they've done today to improve their spelling in general.

Timeline

Devise a timeline to illustrate the events of a book, a scientific process, an historical occasion, a piece of music, a maths formula, the stages of making a cake ... the list is endless.

Thinking skills

Thinking skills are becoming more commonplace in schools today so your students may be familiar with some of the techniques. The *Dfes Standards Site* has a section devoted to thinking skills and the internet is bursting with sites based on thinking and creative thinking. Edward de Bono is famous for a host of thinking strategies that can be taught and used in schools.

Take issues that might be prominent in school (uniform, litter, restricted and compulsory curriculum), local, national and international concerns (local traffic, crime and environmental); build on the thoughts and ideas outlined in the books or take inspiration from the wonderful ideas and questions pupils throw out.

De Bono's *Six Hats* is a thorough and creative approach but can take a while to become familiar with – use for an attentive and enthusiastic class.

Vocabulary tennis

The class tell you the kinds of words they've learned in French, German, Spanish or perhaps even a humanities lesson. Write the categories on the board:

Days and Months
Food and Drink
Countries
Sports and Hobbies
Places in Town

In pairs, students take it in turns to say a word related to the category selected; the winner is the one who doesn't run out of words. With more reserved classes you might start by asking them to practise in their pairs, then go into a class competition, rewarding volunteers credits or similar. You might introduce a three-second rule to keep the game flowing.

Wordsearch or crossword

Using keywords, pupils create a wordsearch or crossword. You will need to give the students a blank grid to work from and explain how to construct a crossword – they are not as easy as they at first appear! To consolidate their learning, encourage students to write clues for the words to be filled in or found.

You'll soon develop and personalize your own individual survival kit as you get a flavour of the type of schools you're in and learn which resources are useful to you. I know that at some of the primary schools I work in I often get a bit of 'free range' time, so I like to have a box with me full of my favourite activities, should I get the chance to use them. At a couple of secondary schools where I have done stints teaching English, I occasionally do one-off English lessons so also have packs of highlighters and editing pens, and maybe a stimulus for a writing activity to hand. I enjoy these opportunities because the lesson is yours, and it's much easier to teach your own thing and the resulting confidence comes across to the pupils.

The lists here are not comprehensive in any sense of the word but a starting point to work from; only you will know what will suit your circumstances and teaching style. I have tried to divide the items into primary and secondary though there are many that overlap and not always obvious ones – I once used a glove puppet to teach Year 8 French! – pick and choose as you see fit.

I tend to drive to schools so can always have my box of tricks to hand but if you're travelling by foot, bike or public transport it's not as convenient. At secondary I pile all of my kit into a large courier bag which is ideal for carting about a big campus.

Secondary

- Cloth – whiteboard rubbers have a habit of being difficult to locate. They are inclined to lurk under papers or get wedged between piles of books. It may seem pedantic but it makes things so much easier to have one to hand. Having to find basic equipment prevents your attention being on the class and stalls the smooth running of a lesson, and wiping the board with your hands is a desperate and grimy measure!
- Hall pass – sometimes used in British schools, I picked up my Hall pass when teaching in the states. Every teacher had one, a square of Perspex engraved with my name, which is given to students who have been given permission to leave the classroom and be out in the 'hall' or corridors. It has a few

benefits: it saves writing notes but also it sort of formalizes a 'one-at-a-time' policy for being out of the room; at primary it also carries a kind of importance that brings with it a more mature standard of behaviour! On the other hand, its novelty factor means it's sometimes best left in the bag!

- Highlighters – this is just a personal preference – I like them for whole-class editing sessions or research activities.
- Keywords – these are one of the most useful resources to have to hand. In the back of the National Strategy for secondary schools folder are lists of subject spelling lists which can be used for most of the word games. Look out for textbooks that contain key concept lists too and jot them down to add to your collection.
- Pencils – as for pens, there are some situations (art, drawing diagrams) when pencils are necessary. A few on standby might relieve the headache of that long, pointless conversations about why someone has turned up to school without the basic equipment.
- Poetry book – everyone will have a favourite but my book for all occasions is *The Family* by John Foster. It is essentially a primary book and full of rhyming poetry, but it is popular for all ages (at a stretch) as everyone recognizes elements of the family relationships depicted. It can provide stimulus for talking about families, about dealing with families, about family memories and stories which can provide the basis for further writing, either prose or poetry, or role plays or sketches. The book is still available second-hand, but books such as *The Puffin Book of Utterly Brilliant Poetry* for KS2, or *The Puffin Book of Fantastic First Poems* for KS1 are great. A quick enlarged photocopy can provide a shared text for literacy, or individual texts to highlight and annotate and classes can explore and analyse the features and structure of a poem or compare two different poems or model their own ideas on a similarly constructed poem. At secondary, I like the *Mersey Sound* (Roger McGough goes down well at all levels) or John Hegley but that's because they are they are personal favourites. With poetry it's best to stick to the stuff you know and love. Reading poems aloud is a simple filler at the end of a lesson or an attention-grabber at the beginning.

- PE kit – at the very least have flat shoes and trousers but trainers and some form of tracksuit bottoms if you're teaching KS2. As a primary specialist you will probably be expected to pitch in and teach PE. Although some teachers often adapt their timetabling so that your day will involve doing more classroom-based activities, you shouldn't rule out having to lead or support a session of PE or dance.
- Red and black pens for registers – finding the right coloured pen to complete manual registers is a hassle you could do without first thing in the morning. Of course you can ask colleagues but it doesn't look professional – keep to hand at all times.
- Red, green and or purple pens for marking, drawing smileys, making positive comments – you will need one of these for yourself and perhaps a few spare for pupils if you are conducting a whole class marking session. I actually now keep a class set (a couple of packets of cheap biros) because they have proved useful over time.
- Spare black or blue biros for individuals without pens. Count the pens in and count them out but don't get too attached – they can get chewed, destroyed or tossed across the classroom. (No, it's not your job to dish out resources to pupils, but trying to run a class where several students have nothing to write with is a nightmare. The first time I heard of teachers giving out pens I was shocked; until that point I had only ever worked in schools where almost all students bought in pens and pencils and the odd one or two that had forgotten could always borrow from a friend. Then I was thrown in at the deep end in a school where the problem was so rife that the students almost expected you to provide pens and I realized that no amount of nagging and moaning would push the lesson further without them. As a permanent member of staff you can work on this issue over time. It is frequently a whole-school concern that students are turning up without the correct equipment, but as a supply teacher you just don't have that influence.)
- Spare lined and plain paper for emergencies – this is usually available close by, but if it isn't you can be left in that horribly

vulnerable position of trying to keep a grip on the class whilst simultaneously searching for paper, not knowing whether to deal with the two boys hurling pencil cases across the room first or find paper for the seven or eight students whining that they need it – they may just be tempted indulge in a spot of flinging themselves if they have to wait unattended for much longer. Have a wodge with you and replace any as you go.

- Stopwatch – stopwatches are great for both primary and secondary for all kinds of activities. In primary (and sometimes enthusiastic Year 7 and 8s), classes really respond to 'beat – the-clock' pack up sessions. Short-timed sessions are a great way to keep classes on track, allowing ten minutes for a paragraph to be written or particular activity to be completed before reporting back. Timed challenges with beanbags or name games are great fillers or drama activities.

  If you have a digital watch that will also either countdown time, or allow you to set an alarm, set reminders for things such as obscure assembly times or lesson changes that you are yet to become familiar with. Mobile phones are very helpful in this way set to a discreet vibrate.

- Supersize pencil case or box to keep pens and pencils, preferably labelled with your name in case it goes amiss.

- Tissues – a travel pack is useful to have to hand for unexpected tears and noses. They save on pupils making drawn-out trips to the toilets just to pick up paper towels or tissue for emergency ink or drinks container leakages, minor abrasions or runny noses.

- Trainers – even if you don't teach PE at secondary you may well be asked to 'be a spare body' in a PE lesson, lead by another teacher. It may just make traipsing around the games field slightly more bearable than it would be in inappropriate footwear.

- Waterproof jacket – there is no end of reasons why it is useful to be equipped with some form of protection against the rain, even if you have stipulated that you don't teach PE. Some campuses are unfeasibly large and you could find yourself on hikes of at least five minutes between departments, registering in the playground before being allowed into the assembly hall, being asked to be a spare body during a PE lesson, where you just get to watch football in the rain while an energetic PE teacher runs the lesson.

- Whiteboard markers – it's worth having a couple of whiteboard markers with you, particularly in secondary where you may find yourself in five or six classrooms in a day. The chances are that none of the handful of markers lying casually on the shelf under the whiteboard actually works properly! Those flowing with an abundance of ink will either be locked in the top drawer of the desk or have gone walkabout.
- *100 Ideas for Supply Teachers*, secondary edition, by Julia Murphy – an invaluable source of practical ideas covering a wide range of subjects at secondary level.

Primary

- Glove puppets or soft toys – use as characters or (temporary) rewards for groups or individuals working well. I've also used glove puppets who whisper the answers into the ears of certain pupils who then have to speak them aloud. Toys and puppets are great fun – children enjoy earning the privilege of spending some time with your furry celebrities. They can also cause a great deal of excitement, hysteria even, so use wisely!
- Juggling balls – these are so incredibly versatile I'm rarely without them. Groups can be entertained by your own juggling prowess (or not!) or someone in the class can have a go; you can have a short, impromptu timed juggling competition to fill in the last five minutes of the lesson or as a reward for working hard. They lend themselves nicely to circle games or teambuilding challenges. One ball on its own can be passed about as a conch enabling the person holding it to speak – very useful for lessons of RE or personal or social type tutor sessions.
- Playing cards – a small but useful item! A pack of cards is by no means essential but can be used for a multitude of activities from selecting orders of volunteers (highest to lowest or

lowest to highest); *Play Your Cards Right* prediction-type activity – starter, plenary or filler; tricks (if you know any); teach an early finisher how to play patience and then get them to teach it on.

- Short story book – I really like *SHORT* by Kevin Crossley-Holland, a book I was introduced to by a supply teaching friend of mine some years ago, because the stories really are short – in one case just one sentence long – which means there's always time to fit one in. With *SHORT* you can speculate about endings, discuss how suspense is engineered and – even in a brief amount of time – have a go at creating your own story of 20–80 words; it's not as easy as it sounds. With such succinct tales, everyone will then have time to read them aloud if they want to. Of course some slightly meatier short stories are also useful for a bit of quiet time to just relax and listen to, but check the length – I once started a favourite Roald Dahl story only to find it was going to take over a week to get through it! Check out too *Short and Shocking* by Maggie Pearson.

- Whistle – great for getting pupils in from break – should you be asked to fill in for an absent colleague's duty, or off the field in a PE lesson. Good for refereeing games, calling large crowds to attention and generally saving your voice. I don't use mine a great deal but there are plenty of times when I wish I'd had one and they're so handy to just slip in a pocket.

- *100 Ideas for Supply Teachers*, primary edition, by Michael Parry – a comprehensive guide of activities to keep primary school classes gainfully occupied, including starters, plenaries and lesson plans.

Checklist

- cloth
- glove puppet or toy
- hall pass
- highlighters

- juggling balls
- keywords
- labelled box or pencil case with your portable equipment
- lined and or plain paper
- marking pen
- PE kit
- playing cards
- poetry book
- register pen
- short story book
- spare pens and pencils for students
- stopwatch
- tissues
- waterproof jacket
- whistle
- whiteboard cloth
- whiteboard pen
- 100 *Ideas for Supply Teachers*

Index